MW01132464

Naval Presence and the Interwar US Navy and Marine Corps

This book examines the US Navy and Marine Corps during the interwar years from a new perspective.

Rather than focusing on the technologies developed, the wargames conducted, or the results of the now famous Fleet Problems, this work analyzes the global deployments of the rest of the US fleet. By examining the annual reports of the Secretary of the Navy, the Chief of Naval Operations, and the Commandant of the Marine Corps over 20 years, the book traces the US ships, squadrons, and fleets conducting naval diplomacy and humanitarian missions, maritime security patrols, and deployments for deterrent effect across the world's oceans. Despite the common label of the interwar years as "isolationist," the deployments of the US Navy and Marine Corps in that period were anything but isolated. The majority of the literature on the era has a narrow focus on preparation for combat and wartime, which provides an incomplete view of the history of US naval power and also establishes a misleading set of precedents and historical context for naval thinkers and strategists in the contemporary world. Offering a wider and more complete understanding of the history of the U.S. Navy and Marine Corps from 1920 to 1939, this book demonstrates the tension between the execution of peacetime missions and the preparation for the next war, while also offering a broader understanding of American naval forces and their role in American and global history.

This book will be of much interest to students of naval and military history, sea power, and International History.

Benjamin Armstrong is an officer in the U.S. Navy and an associate professor of War Studies and Naval History at the U.S. Naval Academy. He is the author or an editor of four books, including *Small Boats and Daring Men: Maritime Raiding, Irregular Warfare, and the Early American Navy* (2019).

Corbett Centre for Maritime Policy Studies Series
Series Editors: Greg Kennedy, Tim Benbow and
Jon Robb-Webb
*Defence Studies Department, Joint Services Command and
Staff College, UK*

The Corbett Centre for Maritime Policy Studies Series is the publishing platform of the Corbett Centre. Drawing on the expertise and wider networks of the Defence Studies Department of King's College London, and based at the Joint Services Command and Staff College in the UK Defence Academy, the Corbett Centre is already a leading centre for academic expertise and education in maritime and naval studies. It enjoys close links with several other institutions, both academic and governmental, that have an interest in maritime matters, including the Developments, Concepts and Doctrine Centre (DCDC), the Naval Staff of the Ministry of Defence and the Naval Historical Branch. The centre and its publishing output aims to promote the understanding and analysis of maritime history and policy and to provide a forum for the interaction of academics, policy-makers and practitioners. Books published under the aegis of the Corbett Centre series reflect these aims and provide an opportunity to stimulate research and debate into a broad range of maritime related themes. The core subject matter for the series is maritime strategy and policy, conceived broadly to include theory, history and practice, military and civil, historical and contemporary, British and international aspects. As a result, this series offers a unique opportunity to examine key issues such as maritime security, the future of naval power, and the commercial uses of the sea, from an exceptionally broad chronological, geographical and thematic range. Truly interdisciplinary in its approach, the series welcomes books from across the humanities, social sciences and professional worlds, providing an unrivalled opportunity for authors and readers to enhance the national and international visibility of maritime affairs, and provide a forum for policy debate and analysis.

Naval Presence and the Interwar US Navy and Marine Corps
Forward Deployment, Crisis Response, and the Tyranny of History
Benjamin Armstrong

For more information about this series, please visit: www.routledge.com/
Corbett-Centre-for-Maritime-Policy-Studies-Series/book-series/CCMPSS

Naval Presence and the Interwar US Navy and Marine Corps

Forward Deployment, Crisis Response, and the Tyranny of History

Benjamin Armstrong

MATTHEW,
THANKS FOR BEING A SOUNDING
BOARD FOR THIS PROJECT AND
FOR YOUR FRIENDSHIP.

Routledge
Taylor & Francis Group

LONDON AND NEW YORK

First published 2024
by Routledge
4 Park Square, Milton Park, Abingdon, Oxon OX14 4RN

and by Routledge
605 Third Avenue, New York, NY 10158

Routledge is an imprint of the Taylor & Francis Group, an informa business

© 2024 Benjamin Armstrong

British Library Cataloguing-in-Publication Data
A catalogue record for this book is available from the British Library

Library of Congress Cataloging-in-Publication Data
A catalog record for this book has been requested

ISBN: 978-1-032-53004-8 (hbk)
ISBN: 978-1-032-53005-5 (pbk)
ISBN: 978-1-003-40967-0 (ebk)

DOI: 10.4324/9781003409670

Typeset in Sabon
by Apex CoVantage, LLC

Contents

Contents

Acknowledgments

Every piece of scholarship has its own unique path, and this monograph is no different. I would like to thank the countless historians who have previously studied this era, including mentors and friends such as C.C. Felker and Trent Hone. Their work so effectively examined the preparations of the U.S. Navy for their next war during the years between the world wars, and they left an opening for someone like me to come along and look at things from a different angle. The U.S. Naval Academy's Nimitz Library, where the research for this work was largely completed, has an amazing staff, including the history librarian Michael Macan, who creates an environment that is easy to work in. I would like to thank my Department Chair, Tom McCarthy, and colleagues in the History Department, including Sharika Crawford, Ernie Tucker, and Matthew Dziennik, for listening to me ramble on about this project over coffees and lunches, and for their wise counsel. Tommy Jamison of the Naval Postgraduate School and J.P. Clark of the Army War College were kind enough to look at early drafts and give me much-needed rudder orders. I owe them all an extra ration of grog.

The team at the Corbett Centre for Maritime Policy Studies and Routledge was fantastic to work with as the project moved toward publication. Well-organized, responsive, and clearly dedicated to producing great books, they earned my deep thanks for helping to make this project become a reality. It is clear to me why they remain an important and respected part of our maritime and naval studies community.

Even with all of these friends, mentors, and colleagues to help, I surely made some mistakes. They are of course mine alone. I look forward to reading the reviews after publication and thank everyone who engages with the history and ideas that are included between these covers.

Finally, I thank Charity for more than two decades of support and friendship. I would not have been able to achieve half of what I have done without your help.

Introduction

In 1922, the United States and the other naval powers of the world completed the negotiations at the Washington Naval Conference. One of the resulting treaties, the Five Power Treaty, which placed arms control limits on capital ships, has generally come to define how naval historians have seen the years between 1920 and the beginning of the Second World War. In American naval history, this interwar era is often cast as two decades of a kind of benign neglect for the U.S. Department of the Navy, correlated to the "doldrum" years in the aftermath of the American Civil War. Overall, Congress saw the Five Power Treaty, which limited the numbers and size of capital ships for the major navies of the world, and the Four Power Treaty, which limited the building of bases and defensive works in the Pacific, as ample reason to trim back funding of the Department and recoup a peace dividend following the First World War. With the election of Franklin D. Roosevelt in 1932 that slowly began to change, but as the Great Depression continued the Navy Department remained conscious of its need for economy and efficiency. At the same time, however, reduced funding resulted in reduced oversight, and the Navy's leadership was largely left to its own devices to experiment and determine the future contours of naval conflict.

The decades of innovation and creative development that resulted, from the introduction of naval aviation to war gaming and war planning initiatives to the development of amphibious warfare, have come to dominate how historians of the American naval forces look at events from 1920 to 1939. This era of innovation is a vital part of understanding the naval past and in particular of understanding the causes of American success in the Second World War.

However, focusing on the work of the Fleet Problems and exercises, the technology development in the United States and testing along the coasts, and the bureaucratic and doctrinal developments that emanated from Washington, D.C., and Newport, Rhode Island, results in a skewed view of American naval forces in the interwar era. This focus by historians tends to give the impression that, after the First World War, the U.S.

DOI: 10.4324/9781003409670-1

Navy returned home to U.S. waters. It creates the impression of something like a "garrison navy" that remained at their home port or made training or practice cruises in the service of the innovative developments of the era. However, this was not entirely true.

During the interwar years, the U.S. Navy remained a globally deployed, operationally active, and strategically vital force conducting peacetime operations. American ships, squadrons, and fleets conducted naval diplomacy and humanitarian missions, maritime security patrols, and deployments for deterrent effect across the world's oceans. Despite the common label of the interwar years as "isolationist," the deployments of the Navy and Marine Corps were global and consistent. The conventional narrative of American naval history focuses on the design and testing of the fleet and the preparation of the officers, sailors, and Marines that would be ready for the next world war. However, navies have missions and responsibilities in peacetime beyond simply the preparation for the next war. From diplomacy to deterrence and from humanitarian missions to security in the maritime world and the protection of commerce, the missions of peace are often overlooked by historians and officers who focus their professional energy on the next potential war.

This myopic focus on combat and wartime provides an incomplete view of the history of American naval power. It establishes a misleading set of precedents and historical context for naval thinkers and strategists in the contemporary world. A wider and more complete understanding of the history of the U.S. Navy and Marine Corps from 1920 to 1939 demonstrates the tension between the execution of peacetime missions and the preparation for the next war while also offering a broader understanding of American naval forces and their role in American and global history.

The Virtuous Cycle

The focus of most scholarship on the interwar years of the U.S. Navy and Marine Corps has been the development of the ships, technologies, and doctrines that would lead to victory against Imperial Japan and Nazi Germany. Sometimes called a "virtuous cycle," this is often described as a relationship between the Naval War College that developed and tested new ideas on the war gaming floors in Newport, the Fleet that conducted the Fleet Problems and exercise sequences to bring those ideas into the "real world" and check their validity, and the General Board and war planning staffs that integrated the ideas into how the United States would potentially fight a future enemy, particularly the Japanese.[1] This is the predominant narrative of the major survey works that cover the expanse of American naval history when they reach the 1920s and 1930s. It is also the subject of a multitude of excellent, deeply researched, and vital books and studies by historians who dive deep into the details of these efforts.

Major survey works of American naval history make the importance of this narrative clear, but, in doing so, they ignore other elements of the history of the era. In Steven Howarth's *To Shining Sea*, the forward-deployed operations of the U.S. Navy and the expeditionary operations of the Marine Corps are hardly mentioned. Chapters Seven, Eight, and Nine cover the era from the end of the First World War to the outbreak of war in Europe in 1939, and the primary focus of the history related is the development of the international tensions between the United States and Japan, the technological and warship development including naval aviation, and the war planning that was conducted.[2] The detailed and highly researched two-volume history of the U.S. Navy by Robert Love focuses on the arms limitations and disarmament, the technological development that resulted from a creative but smaller fleet, and the international politics and economics that would lead to the Second World War.[3] George Baer's *One Hundred Years of Sea Power* focuses on the development in the sequence of Fleet Problems, the fall and rise of American naval shipbuilding, and the creation of "War Plan Orange."[4]

Kenneth Hagan's edited volume *In Peace and War*, often used as a textbook in Naval Reserve Officer Training Corps units, focuses its chapter by Philip Rosen on "The Treaty Navy" and the impacts of naval limitations and technological development.[5] In addition, two chapters in James Bradford's edited textbook *America, Sea Power, and The World*, often used in courses at the U.S. Naval Academy, focus on the era. C.C. Felker's chapter on the Navy of the interwar years focuses on the development of naval aviation, the creation of amphibious warfare doctrine, and the development of war planning.[6] Aaron O'Connell's chapter on the Marine Corps and American Empire contains discussions of some of the period, including the occupations of Haiti, Santo Domingo, and Nicaragua. His examination of the racial and moral questions of empire result in an important analysis of the Marines' expeditions but one that fails to connect them to the Navy's forward presence or the Navy Department's wider operational history of how the deployment of so many forces fit across the era.[7] There is also excellent literature on these elements in specific detail. Books such as C.C. Felker's *Testing American Sea Power*, Albert Nofi's *To Train the Fleet for War*, Trent Hone's *Learning War*, Williamson Murray, Allan Millett's edited volume *Military Innovation in the Interwar Period*, and many others make significant contributions to our understanding of the narrative focused on warfighting development.[8]

The conventional narrative of the interwar years becomes very clear through the examination of these popular, and excellent, survey texts, and detailed monographs. The narrative of developing doctrine and tactics, warship and technological advancement, the creation of naval aviation and amphibious warfare, and how all were connected to both the arms limitations of the 1920s and 1930s, as well as the preparation for a future war, is necessary for the understanding of the U.S. Navy and Marine Corps of the interwar years. It is necessary, but it is not sufficient.

For over two centuries, the Department of the Navy has had to strike a balancing act between the necessity to defend the nation in times of war and the responsibility to protect the national interests in times of peace. It is the reason that the U.S. Constitution separates the Navy from the Army. The Army can be raised in times of war. However, according to the Constitution, Congress must provide for and maintain a navy both in war and in peace.[9] Craig Symonds wrote that, from the earliest days of the republic, this balancing act was critical to the development of naval policy, reflecting that:

> All of President James Monroe's surviving papers on the navy or on naval policy reflect a concern that it efficiently perform two distinct services: first, that it be adequate to cope with the daily problems of a maritime nation—smuggling, piracy, and combating the slave trade; and, second, that it provide the United States with a comfortable degree of readiness in case war should be forced upon the nation.[10]

Despite the focus of many scholars on the preparation for and fighting of wars, the peacetime operations of navies remain important to understanding not only the naval past but also the political, economic, and operational dynamics that can sometimes lead to war in the present and the future.

In the years between 1920 and 1939, the U.S. Fleet had a fluctuating organization that tended to focus on a Battle Fleet with Atlantic and Pacific elements, which remained largely in the western hemisphere and operated out of their home ports. This force prepared for war by training, testing new technologies and weapons, and developing the tactics, techniques, and procedures of the future fleet. However, in addition to this portion of the naval force, there was also a collection of forward-deployed commands that conducted a myriad of tasks including protection of American citizens and business interests, deterrence and showing the flag, naval diplomacy, humanitarian assistance and disaster relief, and maritime security operations. These included the Asiatic Fleet and its subordinate commands the Yangtze Patrol Force and the South China Patrol Force, the Special Service Squadron in the Caribbean and eastern Pacific, and a number of different units in European waters, including the U.S. Naval Detachment, Eastern Mediterranean in the 1920s, and Squadron Forty-T in the 1930s.

Several of these theaters of operations and commands have been written about by historians. The U.S. Navy in China, and the Yangtze Patrol specifically, has had several books and articles written about it, including William Braisted's detailed study *Diplomats in Blue: U.S. Naval Officers in China, 1922–1933*, Kemp Tolley's *Yangtze Patrol: The U.S. Navy in China*, and Bernard Cole's *Gunboats and Marines: The United States Navy in China, 1925–1928*, and articles in both historical and military professional journals.[11] Donald Yerxa's *Admirals and Empire* has several chapters that trace the Special Service Squadron in the era, and Richard Millett's article "The State Department's Navy: A History of the Special Service Squadron, 1920–1940" does the same for the Caribbean based force.[12] The history of the U.S. Navy in European waters after the end of the Great War is covered in detail by William Still's book *Victory Without Peace*, and the operations of Rear Admiral Bristol's forces in the eastern Mediterranean are the focus of Robert Shenk's *America's Black Sea Fleet*.[13] These books all relate the history of naval diplomacy, maritime security, and the other peacetime missions of their units or theaters of operations, but none of them collect the global efforts of the U.S. Navy across two decades into a wider focus.

More Than Warfighters

The purpose of this short monograph is to provide a survey of the U.S. Navy and Marine Corps' forward presence, crisis response missions, and global deployments during the interwar years. This is simply a survey, built on the sources of the Secretary of the Navy's annual report to the President and Congress, and the subordinate reports from the Chief of Naval Operations and the Commandant of the Marine Corps, and supplemented by a handful of other primary sources and the secondary literature. Using the public reports of the Secretary of the Navy (SEC-NAV), the Chief of Naval Operations (CNO), and the Commandant of the Marine Corps (CMC) is complicated for a historian. These reports are clearly institutionally biased, and they are also political documents since they are often used to influence the U.S. Congress in its budgetary debates. However, these elements also make them excellent sources for demonstrating what the Navy and Marine Corps themselves value. It provides a view of what the service leaders thought was most important and what they believed America's elected leaders needed to know. Every single year, some of what was most important for the President and the Congress to learn about was the peacetime operations of the force. Because this monograph is meant as a survey, there are many avenues for further research, which are left open for future historians to examine in deeper detail and with more expansive engagement in the official records, private papers of the participants, and other primary sources.

In order to understand the historic missions of the U.S. Navy and Marine Corps, and to see the sea services' potential roles in the present and the future, a survey like this is important to upend the commonplace wisdom that American naval forces are exclusively focused on war. The conventional narrative of a U.S. Navy that returned home after the end of the First World War and primarily remained in home waters training, testing, and developing new ways of fighting is a false narrative. By examining the official reports of the years from 1920 to 1939, we discover a significant portion of the Navy and Marine Corps which was globally deployed, internationally engaged, and vital to the protection of American interests. These forces were made up of dozens of ships, often reinforced, or supplemented by ships detached from the Battle Fleet when crises required it. They operated in key mission areas that were assigned by the Secretary, missions that the government considered vital to America and its role in the world. For these two decades, American naval forces responded to the tyranny of history, the reality of international crisis and instability, and provided the naval presence required by the American people for their protection in peacetime.

Notes

1 Dale Rielage, "Counting the Cost of Learning: 'Learning War: The Evolution of Fighting Doctrine in the U.S. Navy, 1895–1945'," *Naval War College Review* 72, no. 2 (Spring 2019): 108.
2 Stephen Howarth, *To Shining Sea: The History of the United States Navy, 1775–1998* (Norman, OK: University of Oklahoma Press, 1999), 323–70.
3 Robert W. Love, Jr., *History of the U.S. Navy: Volume One, 1775–1941* (Harrisburg, PA: Stackpole Books, 1992), 524–95.
4 George W. Baer, *One Hundred Years of Sea Power: The U.S. Navy, 1890–1990* (Palo Alto, CA: Stanford University Press, 1994), XXXX.
5 Philip T. Rosen, "The Treaty Navy: 1919–1937," in *In Peace and War: Interpretations of American Naval History, 1775–1978*, ed. Kenneth Hagan (Westport, CT: Greenwood Press, 1978), 221–36.
6 Craig C. Felker, "Finding Certainty in Uncertain Times: The Navy in the Interwar Years," in *America, Sea Power, and the World*, ed. James C. Bradford (Oxford, UK: Wiley and Sons, 2016), 179–92.
7 Aaron O'Connell, "Defending Imperial Interests in Asia and Caribbean, 1898–1941," in *America, Sea Power, and the World*, ed. James C. Bradford (Oxford, UK: Wiley and Sons, 2016), 179–92.
8 Trent Hone, *Learning War: The Evolution of Fighting Doctrine in the U.S. Navy, 1898–1945* (Annapolis, MD: Naval Institute Press, 2018). Craig C. Felker, *Testing American Sea Power: U.S. Navy Strategic Exercises, 1923–1940* (College Station, TX: Texas A&M University Press, 2007). Albert A. Nofi, *To Train the Fleet for War: The U.S. Navy Fleet Problems* (Newport, RI: Naval War College Press, 2010). Williamson Murray and Allan Millet, *Military Innovation in the Interwar Period* (Cambridge, UK: Cambridge University Press, 1998).
9 U.S. Constitution, Article 1, Section 8.

10 Craig Symonds, *Navalists and Anti-Navalists: The Naval Policy Debate in the United States, 1785–1827* (Wilmington, DE: University of Delaware Press, 1980), 223.

11 William Braisted, *Diplomats in Blue: U.S. Naval Officers in China, 1922–1933* (Gainesville, FL: University Press of Florida, 2009). Kemp Tolley, *Yangtze Patrol: The U.S. Navy in China* (Annapolis, MD: Naval Institute Press, 1971). Bernard Cole, *Gunboats and Marines: The United States Navy in China, 1925–1928* (Newark, DE: University of Delaware Press, 1983). Hunter Stires, " 'They Were Playing Chicken'—The Asiatic Fleet's Gray-Zone Deterrence Campaign Against Japan, 1937–40," *Naval War College Review* 72, no. 3 (Summer 2019): 139–58. James Holmes, "Misfit Ships on China's Great River," *Naval History* 33, no. 6 (December 2019).

12 Donald Yerxa, *Admirals and Empire: The United States Navy and the Caribbean, 1898–1945* (Columbia, SC: University of South Carolina Press, 1991). Richard Millett, "The State Department's Navy: A History of the Special Service Squadron, 1920–1940," *The American Neptune* 35, no. 2 (April 1975): 118–38.

13 William Still, *Victory Without Peace: The United States Navy in European Waters, 1919–1924* (Annapolis, MD: Naval Institute Press, 2018). Robert Shenk, *America's Black Sea Fleet: The U.S. Navy Amidst War and Revolution, 1919–1923* (Annapolis, MD: Naval Institute Press, 2012).

I   "A Force for Peace"

The U.S. Navy and Marine Corps of the 1920s

1920

In the aftermath of the First World War, the U.S. Navy found itself in a moment of change and decision. Plans prior to American entry into the war had included the construction of "a navy second to none," and the Naval Act of 1916 put in place a three-year plan to build enough ships to match the Royal Navy. The war itself had intervened. The needs of the conflict and, in particular, the antisubmarine campaign in the Atlantic dictated the construction and the size and shape of the naval force. Following the armistice, Secretary of the Navy Josephus Daniels stated that the Department of the Navy intended to return to the building plan and build a large and balanced fleet that was equivalent to any other navy in the world. He made one caveat. If the United States "entered world concert" and joined an international conference, like the League of Nations that was under negotiation, Daniels believed that it would "be neither necessary nor wise to authorize" the continued construction of such a large fleet. Daniels stated that the goal of the Department of the Navy, regardless of which direction the building plans took, was a U.S. Navy and Marine Corps that was "a force for peace" that would "take its place in the front rank of the champions of international justice and healing."[1]

By 1919, 125 naval vessels had been completed and were being commissioned across the preceding decade. In December 1919, the collier *Jupiter* began conversion into the aircraft carrier *Langley*. The new experimental ship was completed and recommissioned in April 1920. The Department of the Navy's official report highlighted that the British Royal Navy continued to focus on the largest Dreadnought battleships, and the Japanese had initiated the construction of five new capital ships. Studies of captured German submarines were underway, and American recognition that "submarines demonstrated their effectiveness" in the war suggested that they had an important future in the fleets of the world. Even as demobilization continued and troops and ships returned

DOI: 10.4324/9781003409670- 2

home from the fighting in Europe, the technological outlines of the inter-war years were taking shape.[2]

The U.S. Navy in 1920 was organized into three fleets: the Atlantic Fleet, the Pacific Fleet, and the Asiatic Fleet. Both the Atlantic Fleet and the Pacific Fleet conducted exercises during the year. The Atlantic Fleet focused on the Caribbean, based out of Guantanamo Bay, and conducted a mix of general exercises and gunnery practice with port calls. Stops were made in Barbados, Trinidad, and Panama by the battle-ships, and the destroyers spread out more widely across the region. The Pacific Fleet operated off of the California coast and cruised to Hawaii. The early Pacific Fleet exercises included "problems with which our forces might be confronted" and began to suggest the Fleet Problems and exercise system that would come to dominate the work of the Bat-tle Fleet in the coming two decades. Portions of the Pacific Fleet also made cruises to Alaska and along the west coast of Mexico during the year.[3]

The Asiatic Fleet, which had been reduced in size during the war, was rebuilt in 1920 and its independent operations were reestablished. Admiral Albert Gleaves, who had commanded the Cruiser and Trans-port Force in the Atlantic during the war, was placed in command and his fleet grew to 26 ships. These included cruisers, destroyers, mine-sweepers, and auxiliaries. The Yangtze Patrol Force, formally estab-lished in December 1919, was joined by the South China Patrol Force as subordinate units under Gleaves' command. Gleaves conducted naval diplomacy visits to the Galapagos, Marquesas, Tahiti, and Samoa, as well as a circumnavigation of the Philippines to familiarize himself with local waters, followed by visits to Japan and China.[4]

Starting in 1918, the U.S. Army was deployed to Siberia in response to the Russian Revolution and in an effort to protect the Trans-Siberian Railroad, which had been supported by American development and engineers.[5] When Gleaves and the Asiatic Fleet returned to the region in 1920, remnants of the American Expeditionary Force—Siberia (AEF-S) remained in Vladivostok guarding the terminus of the railroad and maintaining an uneasy balance between the local government, the Japanese Army that aspired to take over the region, and the Bolshevik threat. Violence broke out between the forces at Vladivostok in Janu-ary 1920, and Gleaves sailed for the Russian port aboard his flagship the armored cruiser *South Dakota*, with the cruiser *Albany* in company.[6] By the end of the month, the Army transport *Sheridan* arrived to withdraw the AEF-S units. The *South Dakota* and *Albany* landed parties of sailors and Marines to maintain order in Vladivostok as the Army forces pulled back and embarked on their transport, but, as the commander of the White Russian forces sought asylum with the Japanese and Soviet par-tisans entered the outskirts of the town, the Americans completed their withdrawal. With their sailors and Marines back aboard, the cruisers set sail for Japan in early March.[7]

The operations of the Asiatic Fleet began to take shape throughout 1920. The gunboats *Palos* and *Monocacy* cruised portions of the Yangtze River, working to establish security and limit bandit and pirate attacks on American and western-owned shipping and business interests. The gunboats *Elcano* and *Samar* landed forces at Jiujiang[8] in order to help restore order during a riot and protect American merchants in the area. The destroyers *Upsher*, *Rizal*, and *Elliot* assisted with patrols in the lower reaches of the river. Destroyers from Division 2 conducted the patrols of the South China Force, working the coastal waters between Hong Kong and the mouth of the Yangtze. Occasionally, as events dictated, ships were dispatched to respond to wider issues. For example, *Albany* and the cruiser *New Orleans* returned to Vladivostok later in the year to monitor developments there and show the flag, and Gleaves briefly headed inland to Beijing to confer with the U.S. Minister and meet Chinese officials.[9]

In addition to the existing fleets, the U.S. Navy established the Special Service Squadron in the Caribbean in 1920. In 1919, ships from the Atlantic and Pacific Fleets had occasionally been detached for what the Navy often called "police duty" in the Caribbean. With ongoing American interventions and occupations in Haiti and Santo Domingo (today the Dominican Republic), and occasional wider disruptions to American interests, some officers had begun discussing the need for a unit assigned for the purpose rather than ad hoc detachments.[10] In September, after discussions with the State Department, Secretary Daniels formed the Special Service Squadron under the command of Rear Admiral H.F. Bryan. The squadron was initially made up of two divisions of light cruisers and the gunboat *Dolphin* as flagship for a total of nine vessels that were assigned to work with the State Department to provide stability and crisis response in Central and South America, Mexico, and the Caribbean.[11]

Marine Corps operations also continued in the Caribbean in the aftermath of the Great War. The occupation of Haiti had begun in 1915 after the assassination of a series of Haitian Presidents and the Wilson Administration's intervention to provide stability, mostly to protect American economic interests. The Marines took over responsibility for security from local law enforcement, in effect merging Marine units in the country with the Haitian gendarmerie, which was commanded by Marine Lieutenant Colonel Frederic Wise in 1920. The Marines and gendarmerie continued to conduct operations against Haiti's "bandits" throughout the year. Santo Domingo, where the United States had intervened in 1916, was under a similar occupation in 1920 but was reported as largely quiet and secure. Following the end of the war in Europe, the Marine Corps continued its expeditionary deployments to Haiti and

Santo Domingo, reinforcing their units and maintaining expeditionary detachments in Managua, Nicaragua, in Beijing, China, and in Guantanamo Bay, Cuba, and with forward-based units in the Philippines, Guam, and Hawaii. These expeditionary units were in addition to the Marine Detachments deployed aboard Navy ships worldwide.[12]

Even with the two main fleets conducting exercises, the Asiatic Fleet operating in the western Pacific for forward presence and crisis response and the establishment of a patrol squadron for similar operations in the Caribbean, the U.S. Navy still remained actively deployed to European waters in the aftermath of the First World War. In particular, American forces were concentrated in the Adriatic Sea and the eastern Mediterranean in 1920. Rear Admiral Mark Bristol was in command of U.S. Naval Forces in Turkish Waters and in August 1919 had been given the additional diplomatic assignment of serving as the United States High Commissioner to Turkey. Carrying out "various diplomatic, military, and commercial duties, at the same time showing our flag," the naval forces had what Secretary Daniels characterized as "varied and unusual" missions.[13] These included assisting noncombatant evacuations of both Americans and international citizens, as well as the sick and wounded, from the southern ports of the Russian Empire on the Black Sea as Bolshevik advances approached, the movement of State Department diplomats throughout the region, assistance and escort for Red Cross and relief workers, and maritime support to the U.S. government's Food Administration that was attempting to help with the region's widespread postwar food insecurity. The American naval forces helped secure fuel supplies and repair facilities, warehouses, and cargo handling for Food Administration and Committee for Relief in the Near East humanitarian efforts. In addition, Rear Admiral N.A. McCully was dispatched to southern Russia under State Department credentials to serve as an observer, keeping the U.S. government apprised of the rapidly changing situation as the communists continued to expand their power and territory.[14]

Throughout the year 1920, the U.S. Navy and Marine Corps transitioned from fighting the "war to end all wars" to a worldwide deployment model to protect American interests. Like the "constabulary navy" of the 1870s and the 1880s, and the global operations of the "squadron navy" from the 1820s to the 1850s, the American sea services actively deployed for their peacetime responsibilities. Secretary Daniels' desire for a naval "force for peace" in 1920 included the deployment of units forward for crisis response operations and naval presence. The general outlines of these deployments, in the eastern Mediterranean, Western Pacific, and the Caribbean, with ships making diplomatic cruises around the world, laid the keel for the coming decades of American naval deployments.

1921

As the Navy and Marine Corps settled into their postwar roles and missions, eyes remained cast on the future. The development of aviation remained a key effort by the Navy and 1921 introduced both the live-fire exercises in the Chesapeake Bay to test the bombing of naval vessels and also brought the introduction of a Joint Board to study the future of aviation in the services. The new Bureau of Aeronautics was formed in July. Captain William Moffett was confirmed by the Senate and promoted to Rear Admiral as the first Chief of the Bureau.[15] Concerns over postwar budget savings ran high in both the annual report of the new Secretary Edwin Denby and the Chief of Naval Operations Admiral R.E. Coontz. Fleet operations were limited, repair budgets were reduced, and ships were encouraged to increase their "self-maintenance" during the year. In January and February, the Atlantic and Pacific Fleets joined one another at the Panama Canal for the year's "winter maneuvers." Rather than the separate training operations of the previous year, the two fleets held "strategic, tactical, and gunnery exercises" and "engaged in the war game" to prepare the fleet for the future.[16]

Yet, the preparation of the fleet for the possibility of future "national emergency" and war was only a portion of its responsibilities in 1921. Following in the wake of the operations the year prior, naval forces remained forward-deployed and continued to conduct a wide mix of peacetime missions, "engaged continuously in useful and humanitarian enterprises in all maritime waters." Secretary Denby reported the need to continue naval forward deployments as "peaceful instruments for bringing about . . . a better understanding of American aims and ideals."[17]

American naval forces remained deployed to the eastern Mediterranean, Adriatic Sea, and Black Sea conducting humanitarian operations and protecting American interests. During the year, USS *Olympia* and a detachment of destroyers returned to the United States after serving in the Adriatic. Rear Admiral Bristol began establishing the patterns of his mosquito fleet that worked the Adriatic, Black Sea, and eastern Mediterranean. In 1921, he began deploying his destroyers in a system of short-term cruises, more systematically providing assistance to the American Red Cross, as well as the Committee for Near East Relief and the U.S. Food Administration. The ships served as station ships in important ports for a period of time, then passed responsibilities to the next destroyer to arrive, and rotated to a new port. Bristol continuously asked for more ships and was reinforced with destroyers a number of times.[18] In addition to their efforts assisting the humanitarian organizations, Bristol's ships ran noncombatant evacuations out of Crimea as fighting continued in the region and Russian communist forces continued to push south. When the White Russian resistance collapsed, the

American destroyers completed their evacuations and ceased visits to the ports now controlled by the Bolsheviks while continuing wider operations in the region.[19]

Admiral J. Strauss took command of the Asiatic Fleet from Admiral Gleaves in 1921 and maintained the pattern of operations that his predecessor had established. The gunboats of the Yangtze Patrol Force continued movements on the river to protect American citizens and business interests, "preventing strife and protecting persons." In addition, Strauss's Fleet continued the South China Patrol. Ships of the Asiatic Fleet rotated between port calls on the coast of China, assisting the patrol forces, and spending time in Philippine waters conducting gunnery drills and other exercises to maintain their readiness.

Strauss's personal focus fell on the operations on the Yangtze, particularly after Jacob Gould Schurmann, the American Minister to China, reported that "American standing in the Yangtze Valley at the present juncture is undoubtedly at low ebb."[20] Strauss continued an initiative that Gleaves began, pushing Washington to make the Commander, Yangtze Patrol billet, a position for a Rear Admiral. The Asiatic Fleet commanders hoped to ensure that the American naval representative who spent the most time in China was a peer of the other international commanders in Chinese waters. Also, in 1921, the homeports of the gunboats *Elcano*, *Villalobos*, and *Quiros* were formally changed from Manila to Shanghai, making them the only American warships homeported outside of U.S. territory. Strauss spent 26 days on the Yangtze at the start of the summer of 1921, which reinforced for him the complexities of river operations and the political dynamics that his captains would deal with every day. In September, he ordered the Yangtze Patrol Force's supply activity moved from Shanghai further up river to a massive warehouse in Hankou, which would contain "every conceivable thing necessary to keep a gunboat and her people alive and happy."[21] The move solidified that the American mission was going to be long-term and recognized the need for a well-developed and secure supply system for operating deep in another nation's territory. In October, Rear Admiral W.H.G. Bullard arrived as the first flag officer to command the gunboat force.[22]

By the end of the year, American sailors had convoyed Standard Oil ships on the river, protected opium shipments that had been seized by customs inspectors, and exchanged regular small arms fire with bandits and the troops of local warlords on shore. Admiral Strauss reported to the Chief of Naval Operations that "China is torn with strife and dissension . . . Ichang has been looted twice within the year and Wuchang across from Hankou once. Steamers flying foreign flags have been fired on and have been escorted by river gunboats. Landing forces have been landed frequently, and some detachments are still on shore."[23]

While the Asiatic Fleet continued their operations and American naval forces in European Waters maintained a grueling operational schedule, the Special Service Squadron began building its pattern of forward operations based out of the Panama Canal Zone and Guantanamo Bay. Ordered to "promote friendly relations and contribute to the growth of a better understanding" between the United States and the nations of South America and Central America, the squadron conducted port calls and naval diplomacy missions.[24] Crisis response, however, became just as important for the squadron in its first full year of operations. In early 1921, tensions between Panama and Costa Rica flared over a border dispute that kicked off what came to be known as the Coto War. Ships from the Special Service Squadron were deployed to the coast of the two nations, led by the flagship *Dolphin,* including the cruisers *Denver* and *Tacoma* and the gunboat *Sacramento.* These ships offered safety to American citizens and observed both militaries in the conflict.

After diplomatic pressure from the United States, the conflict seemed to end in March, and the squadron's ships returned to their patrols and port visits. *Tacoma* responded to a rumored mutiny on a civilian merchant vessel in La Union, El Salvador. The gunboat *Asheville* cruised the east coast of Mexico as the region struggled with "revolutionary activities." In 1921, the State Department twice asked the Navy to deploy ships as preventative measures to try and head off possible revolutions in Central America, first in Honduras in April and then in Nicaragua in September. In both instances, the arrival of an American warship reassured local Americans and business owners and appeared to "provide a dampening effect" on the possible revolts. When the tensions between Panama and Costa Rica flared again in August, the battleship *Pennsylvania* was sent from the Atlantic Fleet with a detachment of 470 Marines to reinforce the squadron and enforce the results of arbitration over the border. The renewed conflict was soon overcome, and the Marines and *Pennsylvania* returned to the east coast.[25]

Defense of commerce and trade in China, crisis response in the Caribbean, humanitarian assistance, and the protection of noncombatants in the eastern Mediterranean and Black Seas are just a few examples of the peacetime missions of the Navy in 1921. These operations were global, and they mixed the military, economic, and diplomatic elements of naval power, while the Atlantic and Pacific Fleets endeavored to reduce expenses and return the peace dividend that the American people were expecting. At the same time, the Marine Corps maintained their occupation garrisons in Haiti and Santo Domingo, where they worked to develop the *Gendarmerie d'Haiti* and the *Guardia Nacional Dominicana*. Both the First Brigade in Haiti and the Second Brigade in Santo Domingo were visited by the Secretary of the Navy during the year.[26] As discussions of disarmament and the League of Nations focused the attention of the American foreign policy community and the political leadership in Washington, D.C., the Navy and Marine Corps had forward-deployed for global peacetime operations following the end of the First World War.

1922

The Annual Reports of the Navy Department for 1922 began with Secretary Edwin Denby's summary of the Washington Naval Conference and its results, calling it "the greatest outstanding achievement of the past year."[27] Completed just in time for the Secretary to include the results in his message to Congress, the treaties that were signed had two major components. The first, known as The Five Power Pact, was the agreement by Great Britain, the United States, Japan, France, and Italy to limit their capital ships and the size of their fleets based on a tonnage ratio. The United States and Great Britain were authorized equal-sized fleets, with the Japanese slightly smaller, and France and Italy agreeing to the smallest. The second significant agreement, known as The Four Power Pact, agreed to respect the current territorial holdings of Great Britain, the United States, Japan, and France in the Pacific and to freeze the construction of new defensive measures within those territories. This both halted any competition for imperial possessions and attempted to restrict the motives for further competition. While the officer corps in the U.S. Navy largely viewed these agreements with horror, political leaders and the American people saw them as a great success and a harbinger of an era of peace.

Overlooked by the Secretary in his report, and often also overlooked by naval historians in the discussion of the Washington Conference, was an agreement to The Nine Power Treaty. This agreement was signed by the United States, the United Kingdom, Japan, France, Belgium, the Netherlands, Portugal, and China as a promise to respect the territorial integrity of China. In large measure, it ensured the international recognition of the American "Open Door Policy" when it came to trade and international diplomacy with China. However, the treaty contained no enforcement mechanism. Instead, it stipulated that, if a violation of the agreement by one of the signatories was discovered, consultations would be called to determine a way ahead. This openness to diplomacy also resulted in each of the signatories needing to back up their eventual positions, most notably with naval power. The result of the Nine Power Treaty was a highlighting of the relationship between each nation's diplomatic efforts and their naval presence. The Asiatic Fleet became the American enforcement arm of the treaty, not only ensuring the safety and security of American business and civilian interests in China but also necessitating cooperation and collaboration with the other navies in the region to collectively enforce the treaty. It also illustrated the lingering tensions regarding China, the challenges of the continuing civil war and warlordism there and, in particular, of Japan's nascent appetite for expansion.[28]

As the diplomats and naval officers prepared their briefs for the negotiations and then eventually met in Washington, the U.S. Navy remained deployed around the world and in active operations. The Atlantic Fleet remained on the East Coast, spending part of their year in a homeport and a smaller part at Guantanamo Bay, Cuba. However, with reduced funding and limited fuel budgets, the training and maneuvers planned for the fleet to train for future war were canceled, and ships were left to individual gunnery practice and engineering exercises.[29] The Pacific Fleet remained based out of San Pedro, California, and was affected by the same budget limitations as the Atlantic Fleet, resulting in the same focus on individual ship gunnery and engineering. However, the Asiatic Fleet, U.S. Naval Forces in European Waters, and the Special Service Squadron in the Caribbean remained forward-deployed and active throughout the year.[30]

In the Western Pacific, American naval forces remained operational with several missions, including on the rivers of China. China remained a nation in turmoil, with competing warlords and a fluctuating state of civil war, but it was also a nation that attracted a good deal of American business and economic interests. Midway through the year, Admiral Strauss turned over command to Admiral Edwin Anderson, who transferred from European waters. The Yangtze Patrol Force had been formally established under the command of Rear Admiral W.H.G. Bullard and ordered to "protect United States interests, lives, and property, and to maintain the improved friendly relations with the Chinese people."[31] In 1922, Bullard turned over his command of five gunboats to Rear Admiral William Phelps aboard the patrol yacht *Isabel* at Hankou on the lower Yangtze River. He distributed the gunboats along the river, working in cooperation with British forces and shifting their patrol areas in the summer and winter depending on the vessels' draft and the river's changing water levels.[32]

In April 1922, fighting between the forces of General Wu Peifu and Marshal Zhang Zuolin, a pair of Chinese warlords, threatened the American interests in Beijing and the port city of Tianjin, including the American Legation. The Asiatic Fleet's Marine Battalion was formed in the Philippines and deployed aboard the transport USS *Huron* to reinforce the protection offered to Americans in the two cities. Commanded by Major William Wise, they arrived at Taku the first week of May, disembarked, and then moved to Tianjin. They settled into barracks with the U.S. Army's battalions from the 15th Infantry, which were garrisoned in the city. However, by the time the Marines arrived, it appeared that the threat from the fighting had largely passed, and by the end of the month, the battalion reembarked *Huron* and returned to Olongapo in the Philippines.[33]

The U.S. Navy's forces in European waters continued to address the aftermath of the First World War. Commanded by Vice Admiral A.P. Niblack, the postwar drawdown was largely complete, and the remaining force was a European flagship and a force of destroyers commanded by Rear Admiral Mark Bristol, stationed at Constantinople. Bristol served two roles, as the commander of American naval forces in the eastern Mediterranean and the Black Sea but also in a diplomatic post as the State Department appointed "High Commissioner" to Turkey. Bristol's flagship, the patrol yacht *Scorpion*, spent most of the year moored at Constantinople as the squadron made up of eight destroyers and two submarine chasers patrolled the coast of Turkey, the Adriatic, and the Black Sea. In addition to protecting American citizens and commerce, the ships sailed in support of the American Relief Administration's efforts in Russia, which worked to stem the flow of refugees and address food shortages in the aftermath of the war.[34]

Fighting continued in what was left of the Ottoman Empire in the aftermath of the First World War, and Bristol and his destroyer force played a central role in the humanitarian relief efforts that were associated with the fighting. The city of Smyrna (modern-day Izmir) was controlled by the Greeks in the immediate aftermath of the war, with a cosmopolitan population where Muslim Turks lived with a roughly equal number of Christian Greeks, Armenians, and Jewish residents. In September 1922, the Turkish Army approached the city as a part of Mustafa Kamel's effort to unify post-Ottoman territory and create the Republic of Turkey. Greek forces evacuated the city, the final group leaving on 8 September. The Turkish Army moved into the city that evening. Some Turkish forces began to loot the city, and on 13 September, a fire broke out, which spread quickly. This and the violence of the Turkish Army created a refugee crisis as Christian residents turned to the gathered European and American naval forces for help. Bristol coordinated with other naval commanders, and American warships began loading refugees and evacuating them from the city. Through negotiations with the Turks, the Americans gained permission for ten empty Greek ships to moor and load 30,000 refugees. Secretary Denby reported to Congress that the "story of the rescue work of these young sailors will form one of the brightest pages in the history of our Navy."[35]

In the Caribbean, the Special Service squadron was made up of five cruisers that patrolled the West Indies. As with the Black Sea and Mediterranean destroyers, these ships regularly made port calls to check on the safety and security of American citizens and conduct diplomacy. In addition, the Navy Hydrographic office sent USS *Hannibal* on a survey expedition of the east coast of Nicaragua and continued operations on the coast of Cuba near Guantanamo Bay.[36] In late 1921, the Third Battalion of the 5th Marines had deployed to Balboa, Panama, during a dispute over the Panama-Costa Rica border, but the forces were withdrawn after several weeks.[37] The Marines continued the occupations of Haiti and the Dominican Republic. This included training centers, hospitals manned by the Navy's medical personnel, and aviation squadrons for observation and air support.[38] Finally, the Marine guard at the American legation in Managua, Nicaragua, continued its reinforced operations at the request of the Nicaraguan government. The Marines maintained their own secure communications by running a radio station, and during an attempted revolt in May 1922, Marines assisted in the protection of the city.[39]

1923

A year after the formalization of the treaties that came from the Washington Conference, the U.S. Navy began the elaborate fleet exercises that would become a hallmark of the interwar years and the focus of much scholarship. In total, 165 vessels took part in the maneuvers in 1923, with 37,000 sailors and Marines conducting them under the command of 2,200 officers. These were the largest exercises that the U.S. Navy had ever conducted and ranged through the Caribbean and along the Pacific coast of Panama.[40] A great deal was learned. However, there were more deployments and wider operations throughout the world.

In 1923, the Navy commissioned several new Light Cruisers, ships designed for scouting with long ranges and built for oceanic operations. In conducting their shakedown cruises, these ships were also given a second task of wider naval diplomacy. USS *Milwaukee* left Puget Sound for a visit to Australia and South Seas islands in July, a month after her commissioning. USS *Richmond* left Newport, Rhode Island, for a cruise along the coast of Africa and visits to St Helena, Ascension Island, and South American ports during her return voyage. USS *Detroit* departed Norfolk, Virginia, in September for the Mediterranean visiting ports as far as Alexandria, Egypt. Plans were also underway for the USS *Concord*, *Cincinnati*, and *Raleigh* to depart on naval diplomacy shakedown cruises early in 1924, with *Trenton*, *Marblehead*, and *Memphis* to follow sometime later in the year.[41]

The maritime security operations and patrols of the gunboats that made up the Yangtze River Patrol Force continued throughout 1923. The small ships conducted counterpiracy operations, saving a passenger steamer from a pirate attack and recapturing a number of oil-carrying junks, and returning them to their American owners. Officers of the patrol also played a role in local diplomacy, helping to negotiate

between warlords and their armies in order to protect civilian populations. Despite all the efforts of the Patrol Force, the American Chamber
of Commerce in Shanghai complained to the Secretary of the Navy that
the United States still was not doing enough to protect American commerce in Chinese waters. The trade between the United States and China
in 1923 totaled over $346 million, which gave them a voice in Wash-
ington, D.C. The details of some of their complaints were legitimate,
and the age and deep draft of the American gunboats (some of which
were captured from the Spanish in the War of 1898) kept them from
patrolling the upper reaches of the river during part of the year. The
experience of the older and difficult-to-maintain vessels caused the Navy
Department to request funding for the construction of purpose-designed
river gunboats, telling Congress that "the use of worn out, improperly
equipped, and inefficient vessels on a river, in addition to failing to render the actual protection required by American interests, does not reflect
credit on our flag nor add to our prestige."[42]

In September 1922, a massive earthquake and tsunami struck the coast
of Japan in the vicinity of Tokyo and Yokohama. Through the fall of
1922 and early in 1923, the U.S. Navy responded to the humanitarian crisis, deploying ships and resources from the Asiatic Fleet to the coast. The
first to arrive were the destroyers of Division 38, led by the new Wickes
class destroyer USS *Stewart* that had recently arrived in the Pacific.[43] The
ships and their crews conducted reconnaissance and sent information on
conditions and the needs of the Japanese back to the Philippines, where
the Asiatic Fleet was headquartered.

President Harding authorized the Asiatic Fleet to purchase whatever
Admiral Anderson deemed necessary to "give all possible aid" to the
Japanese. Supply ships rushed food, medicine, and logistical support
to Japan's ports.[44] A field hospital was constructed, at the request of
the Japanese government, where Navy doctors and nurses treated hundreds of injured and ill survivors. The destroyers shuttled between Japanese ports, accounting for Americans in the country and providing them
and American businesses assistance, as well as carrying representatives
of the Red Cross for assessments of local conditions and the continuing
need for support. The American warships evacuated American citizens,
while sailors and Marines went ashore to recover as much as they could
from destroyed American Consulates and help the State Department
reopen operations in a camp that the Marines constructed. They continued to provide medical aid, distribute supplies, and help with logistics and off-loading of ships as they arrived with aid. In an era when
naval scholars often focus on the rise of the Japanese Imperial Navy and
potential tensions in the Pacific, Secretary of the Navy Denby pointed
out to Congress that "within the four seas, all men are brothers" and the
Navy took great pride in their humanitarian efforts.[45]

Japan was not the only area of humanitarian assistance, either. In November 1922, another earthquake and tsunami struck the opposite side of the Pacific, ravaging the coast of Chile. The cruisers USS *Cleveland* and *Denver* were the closest ships, and they pulled into the Panama Canal Zone to load emergency provisions, medical supplies, and clothing. Sailing for Huasco, Chile, the ships delivered the aid and discovered hundreds of homes destroyed. Sailors worked to move the supplies ashore and distribute the lifesaving aid to the Chilean people.[46]

In 1923, the full aftermath of the burning of Smyrna was understood, and the American destroyer force under Rear Admiral Bristol grew from six destroyers to 20. In total, over 250,000 Greeks and Armenians had been evacuated by American ships or by other vessels under American protection. As fighting continued in Turkey, communications were severed from many cities, and American destroyers took up moorings in Trebizond, Samsun, Constantinople, Athens, Smyrna, and other ports, and made a radio chain in order to pass messages and keep American businesses and State Department representatives informed and in communication. By October 1923, the situation was stabilized, and the force was reduced back to six destroyers plus a tender, supply ship, and Bristol's station ship *Scorpion*.[47]

The Marine Corps remained actively engaged in the occupations of Haiti and the Dominican Republic in 1923, and the reinforced legation guard remained in Nicaragua. The year saw the reduction of forces in both nations, with Marines withdrawn from several districts in Haiti and security handed over to the Haitian security forces. Marines continued to patrol in the central region of the country, with the Commandant reporting that "Cacoism and organized banditry are things of the past." In addition, the Commandant reported that the Marine Corps had completed its building programs in Haiti, with the necessary bases and substations complete, and he described increased training for Marines joining the mission in "indoctrination of the men with regard to their contact with the natives," suggesting attempts to improve local relations.[48]

1924

China remained the center of focus for the operations of the Asiatic Fleet in 1924, with continued demands on the Yangtze Patrol Force and other ships in the region. Admiral Thomas Washington had taken command from Admiral Anderson in October 1923. American merchant interests regularly complained to the Navy Department and their representatives of insufficient support on the rivers and ports of China. In order to help address the operational requirements the minesweepers *Pigeon* and *Penguin* were brought out of mothballs at Pearl Harbor and sent to join the patrol force, but they were too deep draft to access all the areas in need of patrol. In Washington, the Navy Department reminded Congress again of the need for purpose-built riverine patrol ships. The reality was that the Patrol Force was simply busy. During a single week in June 1924, 32 international merchant ships entered or departed Chongqing, most of them requiring some form of protection during their voyages. The Patrol Force also reported increasing cooperation with European naval powers in and around Shanghai and in addressing security concerns of international communities near Beijing.[49]

At the start of the year, the Chinese leader Sun Yat-sen, President of the Republic of China, which controlled much of the southern part of the country, threatened the western trading settlement known as Canton in Guangzhou. Guangzhou had been under western international control for almost a century, and his threat of seizing the customs house and local law enforcement was seen as a great threat to American and international business interests. The Asiatic Fleet deployed six destroyers to Guangzhou to join the naval forces of other powers in reinforcing international control. The strong response from the western navies caused Sun Yat-sen to back down from his threat and the economic independence of Guangzhou as a western-controlled port remained secured.[50]

In 1924, the American perspective was that Europe had largely quieted. The Mediterranean command retained its six destroyers, primarily operating in the east as in previous years. The cruiser *Pittsburgh* served as the flagship of the reduced force in European waters. In the Atlantic and the Pacific, naval vessels supported an attempt by U.S. Army aviators to fly four aircraft around the world. Destroyers and cruisers were deployed in both oceans to move support equipment, provide radio communications relays and navigation assistance, and provide search and rescue if necessary. While providing this assistance to the Army, the cruiser *Richmond* was dispatched to search for an Italian crew, which was attempting to fly across the Atlantic and had gone missing. After 60 hours of searching, *Richmond* found and recovered Lieutenant Antonio Locatelli and his crew from the North Atlantic.[51]

American naval forces in the Caribbean, under the organization of the Special Services Squadron, had an operationally busy year with crisis responses missions to Mexico and Honduras. Mexico had been wracked by political instability, with occasional violence, beginning in 1910. In 1924, Washington became concerned about what appeared to be an imminent outbreak of violence against the government of the former general Álvaro Obregón in Mexico City. With concerns about American lives and business interests in the balance, the light cruiser *Richmond*, recently returned from its diplomatic deployment along the African and South American coasts, was sent to Tampico. The cruiser *Omaha* was joined by destroyers *Corry*, *Farenholt*, *Hull*, *MacDonough*, *Shirk*, and *Sumner,* and the small squadron sailed for Vera Cruz. Conditions stabilized after several weeks, and the ships returned to the previously assigned duties.

A presidential election in Honduras raised the specter of violence; in January and February, the Special Services Squadron was also deployed to contend with the potential threats that it created for American interests. The cruiser *Milwaukee* had returned from its diplomatic deployment to Australian and the islands of the South Pacific and was in the process of joining the west coast's Light Cruiser Division when it was redeployed south to Amapala, Honduras, in the Gulf of Fonseca on the Pacific Coast. It landed a force of sailors and Marines who headed inland to reinforce the American embassy in Tegucigalpa and remained there for three months as conditions stabilized. On the east coast of Honduras, the destroyers *Billingsley* and *Lardner* transported Marines to La Ceiba to reinforce the cruiser *Denver* before returning to their patrol duties in the Caribbean. In April, *Richmond* transported the State Department's Special Commissioner to the Dominican Republic Sumner Welles from Santo Domingo to La Ceiba as a diplomatic representative to help negotiate a solution to the political tensions over the Honduran election. Welles crossed Honduras to the West Coast and hosted a negotiation between the competing parties aboard *Milwaukee* in the Gulf of Fonseca. By the end of the month, the negotiations appeared to be a success, the sailors and Marines in Tegucigalpa returned to *Milwaukee*, and the ships departed Honduran waters.[52]

The Hydrographic Office of the Department of the Navy also continued operations in the Caribbean, primarily using Special Service Squadron ships. Work continued on a survey around Guantanamo Bay, Cuba. USS *Hannibal* was joined by several auxiliaries in conducting wider surveys in Cuban waters along the southwest coast of the island, with aerial overflight and mapping provided by the air units attached to the Scouting Force. USS *Nakomis* concentrated its scientific and charting efforts along the coast of Haiti for most of the year before moving to the north coast of Cuba to begin operations near Cardenas and eastward. Eight other naval ships participated in surveying and mapping operations around the Caribbean and from the west coast of South America to Alaskan waters.[53]

Operations of the Marine Corps continued in both Nicaragua, with the legation guard, and maintenance and operation of the communications station, as well as the occupation of Haiti. Commandant Lejeune reported a year of overall success in Haiti, claiming that banditry had largely been eliminated, and the "well-trained, highly efficient" Haitian gendarmerie took over most security requirements in the country and had even fielded a rifle team for the Olympics. The year also brought to a close the occupation of Santo Domingo. The Marine operations in

Santo Domingo had begun in 1916 in parallel with the Haitian occupation. According to Lejeune, the Marines had endeavored over the years to establish security and train a local constabulary, and foreign capital had returned with investments that employed many Dominicans, primarily in the sugar industry. With the establishment of a provisional local government in late 1922, by March 1924, Brigadier General Harry Lee, the appointed military governor of the occupation, determined that the Marines' mission was complete and began leading the withdrawal.[54]

1925

The pattern of overseas deployments and naval presence for the U.S. Navy during the 1920s was well established by the mid-decade. The organization of forward-deployed forces remained consistent, with the Asiatic Fleet continuing to support the Yangtze Patrol Force, a destroyer force in the Mediterranean providing continuous operations in European waters, the Special Services Squadron working throughout the Caribbean and the coast of South America, and ships of the Naval Transportation Service and Hydrographic Office carrying out missions around the world. Four new light cruisers were on shakedown cruises with associated naval diplomatic missions in 1925. *Raleigh* completed her cruise to the Baltic and Northern European ports at the very start of the year. *Trenton* also returned from its circumnavigation of Africa, having departed in late 1924. *Marblehead* sailed for the Mediterranean, visiting European and North African ports. *Memphis* conducted a short shakedown to the Caribbean, visiting Trinidad to support a memorial commemoration of Oliver Hazard Perry, before heading to the Pacific to join the ships that were completing the 1925 fleet exercises.[55]

   The 1925 Fleet Exercises centered around the Hawaiian Islands, the Battle Fleet, and the Scouting Fleet joining U.S. Army units in wider joint defensive and offensive exercises, and were followed by naval diplomacy missions. At the end of the maneuvers, at the start of July, the Battle Fleet was joined by a division of light cruisers from the Scouting Fleet and departed Hawaiian waters to cross the rest of the Pacific on a diplomatic and presence cruise to Australia, New Zealand, and the islands of the South Pacific. The Secretary of the Navy reported the cruise, which lasted from July through September, as "one of the outstanding features of the work of the Navy during the last year." The ships carried nearly 25,000 sailors and officers throughout the South Pacific, making port calls and conducting diplomatic events. The Secretary quoted the opinion page of one New Zealand newspaper, which said after visits to ports along their coast, "we are, therefore, not only friendly to our departing visitors, but exceedingly proud of our American cousins and anxious to see more of them and hear more about them."[56] On the return voyage, the cruisers of the detached Scouting Fleet division, made port calls in the islands of the South Seas, and crossed through the Panama Canal in September to rejoin the Scouting Fleet in the Atlantic area.[57]

For most of the year, the Asiatic Fleet was commanded by Admiral Washington and continued a high operational tempo in the waters in and around China. American mercantile interests continued to demand greater protection from bandits and warlordism, and Congress finally funded the six purpose-designed gunboats that the Navy Department had been requesting for years in order to reach the shallower parts of the Yangtze and its tributaries. More than just the gunboats and minesweepers of the Patrol Force, almost the entire Asiatic Fleet was deployed to Chinese rivers or coastal ports at some point in a year filled with "political disturbances."[58] The State Department largely maintained a policy of noninterference. The Navy followed this lead, in some measure because of the lack of ships and also the lack of Marines for landing parties to influence events ashore. The Marine Corps had slightly over 1600 Marines deployed across the Pacific, in small garrisons in Beijing, Shanghai, Guam, and the Philippines, as well as in shipboard detachments on the larger warships. Spread thin, however, they were largely unavailable for work up the rivers with the Yangtze Patrol. The gunboats did the best they could, responding to both the instability caused by warlords vying for power and criminal and piratical elements in the riverine environment.[59]

In the early summer of 1925, unrest broke out in Shanghai, which required a direct response by the Asiatic Fleet. Chinese students and laborers conducted a protest march through the International Settlement after a worker had been killed while on strike. The crowd ended up surrounding a police station where several arrested protestors had been taken, and Chinese police fired into the crowd, killing 12 and wounding 17. A general strike was called by local labor groups, and the Shanghai government asked the international community for landing parties and reinforcements to protect public utilities and government buildings from the riots they expected to develop. Three American destroyers were already in port at Shanghai, and six other destroyers, the gunboat *Sacramento*, and the collier *Jason* with 125 Marines embarked were dispatched to the city immediately. By 8 June, there were 445 Americans ashore as a part of a 900-man international protection force, and six destroyers, six gunboats, and the collier with a total of another 1,000 sailors aboard and available. Rear Admiral McVay, the commander of the American Yangtze Patrol Force, was placed in overall tactical command of the combined multinational force by the representatives of the foreign communities in Shanghai.[60]

The international force in Shanghai was generally able to keep a lid on tensions. The unrest spread slowly, with minor issues developing in other small towns along the river and the southern coast. The most dangerous location for the spread of unrest was in Guangzhou, but the international naval force gathered there was able to contain the threat. Most Chinese ire appeared directed at the British, and the American naval forces, merchants, and missionaries were largely spared the worst of Chinese anger. By the end of the summer, tensions had been reduced enough that the landing forces were removed from Shanghai, and American patrols and operations returned to their previous routine. Admiral Washington turned over to Admiral Clarence Williams in October as the Fleet returned to a regular patrol schedule.[61]

In European waters, the cruiser *Pittsburgh* continued to serve as flagship, joined by Destroyer Division 26 in 1925. Regular cruises were along the Mediterranean with port calls in both Europe and North Africa. *Scorpion* remained the station ship for Constantinople in 1925, serving the missions of Rear Admiral Bristol who continued in his dual State Department and Navy role as a High Commissioner to Turkey, regularly sailing from its anchorage for other Black Sea and Adriatic ports. The destroyers working in the eastern Mediterranean worked in continuing support to the refugee and humanitarian challenges that were the result of the post-Ottoman strife in Turkey. The Near East Relief organization, a nongovernmental organization founded in 1915 in the aftermath of the Armenian genocide, sent a letter to the Secretary of the Navy as Navy Day approached in October 1925 to express their thanks for all the humanitarian work and the "constant and alert service" of the Navy's European forces over the years following the end of the First World War. The safe movement of refugees, the protection of the defenseless, security for American citizens, and businesses and charities were all lauded by Near East Relief.[62]

Following a busy year in 1924, events in the Caribbean were relatively quiet for the Special Service Squadron in 1925. At the end of 1924, the battleship USS *Utah* carried General John Pershing and Admiral J.H. Dayton, commander of the special service squadron, and a diplomatic delegation to Peru to join in the commemoration of the Battle of Ayacucho. Arriving at Valparaiso, the delegation traveled across the South American continent by rail and joined diplomatic events in Buenos Aires. *Utah* crossed through the Straits of Magellan and met the delegation on the other side of the continent in Montevideo.[63] They then sailed the coast north, making port calls in Rio de Janeiro, Trinidad, La Guaira, and Havana, before returning home in March 1925. Ships of the squadron also continued their work for the Hydrographic Office, including *Hannibal*, *Nokomis*, and *Niagara* working around Cuba and in the Gulf of Mexico.[64]

At the end of June, Santa Barbara, California, was struck by an earthquake and the 11th and 12th naval districts along the west coast responded, as well as the ships of the Midshipmen's practice squadron that was at sea for summer training. Eagle class patrol craft *34* was the first vessel to arrive along with the Navy tug *Koka*, both of which assisted navy medical personnel in establishing aid stations. The battleship *Arkansas*, cruising with midshipmen, arrived on the 30th and was soon joined by *McCawley*, *Pinola*, *Algoma*, and *Sonoma* from San Francisco. Landing parties went ashore to establish shore patrols and assist local law enforcement. Teams from the ships and the naval district construct a temporary radio station in order to improve communications. A battalion of Marines arrived from San Diego to assist with the shore patrols, serving through the rest of July. The ships departed after only a few days, as the damage was limited and the Marines' assistance to law enforcement was deemed sufficient.[65]

The Marine brigade maintained in Haiti continued to provide officers to the Haitian Gendarmerie, which the Commandant reported as providing security and "protection of life and property." In Nicaragua, following the withdrawal of the Marine occupation force in the Dominican Republic the previous year, the reinforcement of the legation guard was ended, and the Marines embarked USS *Henderson* at Corinto and departed the country. Marines remained in Shanghai, China, cooperating with other international forces to maintain security in the large international community.[66]

In the year that Americans were greeted in their morning newspapers with the news of the end of the Scopes Monkey Trial and were reading F. Scott Fitzgerald's new book *The Great Gatsby*, the navy was deployed all over the world. The American Battle Fleet continued its interwar exercises with Fleet Problem V for the first time including an aircraft carrier as USS *Langley* joined the operations and overshadowed the maritime security operations, diplomatic missions, disaster relief, and protection of American citizens by naval units worldwide. From the western Pacific to the eastern Mediterranean, and across the Caribbean, forward-deployed navy ships and Marine Corps units continued to respond to the crises of the moment and remained forward-deployed to advance American peacetime interests.

1926

Following the joint maneuvers in Hawaii in 1925, the 1926 Fleet Problem returned to the Panama Canal and again included the Army in the exercises. The Navy also conducted its own dispersed exercises in the Caribbean, on the Atlantic coast, and on the North Pacific coast. In addition to the Fleet Problems and Joint Maneuvers to prepare the Battle Fleet and Scouting Fleet for war, the Navy's forward-deployed ships remained globally engaged to conduct presence missions and respond to the needs of American leaders and citizens abroad. After years of instability in China and the Caribbean world, American forward deployed naval forces appeared to find a footing in 1926. Minor threats and crises continued to bubble to the surface, but the deterrence and the rapid responses provided by American presence appeared to keep the challenges at the lower end of the spectrum of violence overall.[67]

In the Asiatic Fleet's area of operations, instability in China continued to drive operations and the deployment of the Fleet. The Yangtze Patrol Force found itself overwhelmed by the number of violent outbreaks that threatened American interests, and a squadron of destroyers was dispatched from Subic Bay to support the Patrol Force's operations. As in previous years, the American Chamber of Commerce in China continued to express its concerns to political leaders in Washington about insufficient resources dedicated to their protection. The Northern Expedition, the name given to a push by Chiang Kai-shek's Kuomintang toward Beijing, concerned Americans in China but was, for the most part, contained as fighting between Chinese factions. When the Kuomintang attempted to establish control of the traffic on the Yangtze, the Americans refused to comply, and Chiang Kai-shek backed down. However, each of the individual threats and events that the Asiatic Fleet responded to remained relatively minor.[68] The age of the gunboats of the Patrol Force continued to concern the Chief of Operations. The *Helena* and *Pampanga* were inspected and ruled not fit for sea. The anticipated completion of the purpose-designed six gunboats being built in Shanghai and scheduled for completion in 1927 and 1928 raised the expectation of improved operational capabilities in the near future.[69]

In the European theater, the ships under the command of Vice Admiral G.H. Welles were replaced with a rotation of fresh ships. The light cruiser *Pittsburgh* was replaced by *Memphis* as the flagship, and Destroyer Division 27 was relieved by Destroyer Division 25. As had been the norm throughout the postwar years, the Commander of Naval Forces in European Waters continued to collaborate explicitly with the State Department via European embassies. Rear Admiral Bristol remained "dual-hatted" as both the commander of naval forces in the eastern Mediterranean and the State Department's High Commissioner to Turkey, with *Scorpion* continuing to steam between Constantinople and other Turkish ports with occasional visits by the ships of Destroyer Division 25.[70]

The Special Service Squadron remained busy with a variety of missions in the Caribbean and Central and South America. Toward the beginning of the year, the squadron supported diplomatic missions in the western hemisphere. After returning from the commemoration of the Battle of Ayacucho in the previous year, General Pershing sailed south again aboard *Rochester* from Key West for Arica, Chile. *Rochester* served as the initial flagship for his diplomatic mission for the Tacna-Arica arbitration. The arbitration was an international effort to resolve a long-standing dispute over the northern border of Chile with Peru following the Pacific War from 1879 to 1882. The treaty of Ancon, which ended the war, established a plan for an election in a decade's time where the population in the provinces of Tacna and Arica would vote as to whether they would remain under Chilean rule. Pershing and a delegation were dispatched aboard *Rochester* to represent the United States in the election monitoring efforts associated with the plebiscite.[71] The cruiser *Rochester* was relieved by *Denver* as the flagship after reaching the coast of Chile, and *Cleveland* and *Galveston* also supported the diplomacy and port calls at different points in 1926. The observer mission returned from Chile to the Panama Canal Zone in June aboard *Denver* and *Cleveland*.[72] USS *Hannibal* continued its survey mission along the south coast of Cuba covering 1675 square miles of ocean space. On the north coast of Cuba, the USS *Nakomis* continued its work westward past Matanzas, covering 600 square miles. The Hydrographic office completed the charts of the areas that each ship had surveyed the year prior. In addition, USS *Niagara* worked a section of the coast of Venezuela covering 40 miles of coastline before heading for Philadelphia for a shipyard repair period.[73]

Following the withdrawal of the Marine reinforcement of the legation Guard in Managua in 1925, Nicaragua again experienced turmoil in 1926. In June, the light cruiser *Tulsa* sailed into the port of Bluefields to provide stability to American interests and remained there for several weeks. Not long after she departed, however, instability rose again in August, and *Tulsa* returned to the east coast of the country and *Rochester* to the west coast. They were joined by their fellow light cruisers *Galveston* and *Denver*, and a pair of destroyers. The force remained in the area from August through October.[74] While sailors and Marines from the ship's detachments were providing stability in Nicaraguan ports, patrolling the streets for security, the Marines continued to draw down their forces in Haiti and consolidated the force to two bases at Port au Prince and Cap Haitien.[75]

The Navy was again called upon for humanitarian relief inside the United States when a pair of hurricanes struck Florida in September. The first storm struck Miami directly, passing over the peninsula and then heading for Pensacola. The department reported that, while there luckily was no loss of life at the Pensacola Naval Station, the property damage on the base was significant. The initial estimate was damage totaling at least $1,000,000. Around Miami, the Sixth and Seventh Naval Districts provided aid and medical support, and sent naval personnel to contribute to the rescue work and assist local law enforcement. The Navy tug *Bagaduce* was the only ship in the era and promptly sailed from Key

West for Miami to help clear obstacles. The tug *Umpqua* sailed from Charleston, and the two navy vessels collaborated with the local Coast Guard units who also helped bring in naval personnel and aid.[76] The storm at Miami and Pensacola was quickly followed by another hurricane that struck the coast of Cuba. Loss of life and damage were particularly heavy near the Isle of Pines, which had a high population of American expatriates in the area. The light cruiser *Milwaukee* and the destroyer *Goff* were sent in response by the Special Service Squadron from Guantanamo Bay and began to render aid. *Milwaukee's* pair of scout aircraft flew ahead of the ships to bring immediate medical aid and provide reconnaissance of the damage. The ships remained in the area providing relief until they exhausted their supplies.[77]

1927

Five years after the signing of the Five Power Pact and the Four Power Pact at the Washington Naval Conference, the world's leading naval powers returned to the negotiating table in Geneva. The United States, the United Kingdom, and Japan sent delegations to the Three Power Conference on Limitation of Naval Armaments in June. Working through August, the negotiators this time had much greater representation from the naval officer corps of each of the countries. By August, it was clear that a further agreement between the three countries was not going to happen, and the negotiations broke up without any agreements.[78] Fleet problems dominated the work of the Battle Fleet and Scouting Fleet as was the norm in the interwar era. As in prior years, the Battle Fleet began the year with exercises on the west coast, this time in the vicinity of Seattle and the Bremerton Naval Station. Following west coast operations, the Battle Fleet transited the Panama Canal and conducted joint maneuvers in the Caribbean with the U.S. Army and other naval units. The Navy hosted the United States Fleet Concentration in Norfolk in June 1927 before the Battle Fleet returned to the Pacific.[79]

The readiness of the Battle Fleet and Scouting Fleet for war and the continued development of doctrine and war plans through the Fleet Problems remained a priority for the Secretary of the Navy in 1927. However, those missions are listed in parallel with the need to ensure "the protection of Americans in the Far East," "the protection of Americans in Central America," and, finally, "the maintenance of a European and Near Eastern Squadron." The Secretary highlighted the "close cooperation between representatives of the Department of State and of the Navy," as a key element of maintaining the missions he listed.[80]

Operations of the Asiatic Fleet increased in and around Chinese waters in 1927, with the Secretary reporting that the year "has been one of intense naval activity." By the end of the year, the entire Asiatic Fleet was in Chinese waters, and Washington had ordered three additional cruisers from Light Cruiser Division 3, two transports, and an extra brigade of 4,400 Marines to the western Pacific. Reinforcements were moved forward from Guam to Manila, additional Marines were sent from California, and 20 Marine Corps aircraft were forward-deployed to the Philippines. The Chinese Civil War accelerated, and the naval forces had to deal with increasing refugee flows, demands for humanitarian assistance, the support of American business interests, and the protection of American lives. The Secretary reported that operations "required the greatest amount of tact, patience, and calm judgment" as commanders dealt with a war raging around them while trying to maintain American neutrality. The focus remained on protecting the lives of Americans and innocents, leading, in some cases, to the abandonment and destruction of American property.[81]

For the most part, American officers were able to resist the need to use force and instead relied on negotiation and diplomacy. Landings were conducted by sailors when USS *Asheville* arrived at Yangjiang to protect American missionaries, and USS *Sacramento* landed a force at Guangzhou in December in order to protect local businesses. Both landing operations were short-lived and resulted in a return to stability.[82] Marine reinforcements from the 4th Marine Regiment arrived at Shanghai in February and moved ashore in March. At the same time, the troops of the National Revolutionary Army assaulted Nanjing and the large international settlement there. The Navy reported that "there can be no doubt that this attack on foreigners, including Americans, was premeditated, carefully planned, well organized, and efficiently executed by organized troops." The U.S. Navy and Royal Navy collaborated in their response, drawing ships close to shore and initiating a naval gunfire mission to clear the area around the location of the American Consul's offices, an effort that the Secretary reported "prevented a possible wholesale massacre" and facilitated the safe evacuation of the international community in the city.[83] Marine reinforcements were called for, and the 6th Regiment and Third Brigade Headquarters sailed from San Diego. Brigadier General Smedley Butler, in command of the Third Brigade, took command of the Marines ashore, and as reinforcements arrived, they were split between Shanghai and Tianjin.[84]

In the Mediterranean and European waters, the Navy continued operating in close cooperation with the State Department. After a year of being forward-deployed, the cruiser *Memphis* and the Destroyer Division 25 were relieved by the USS *Detroit* and the Destroyer Division 38. *Memphis* happened to be departing Europe as the celebrations of Charles Lindbergh's transatlantic crossing were winding down, and President Calvin Coolidge assigned the cruiser to bring the returning hero, and his aircraft the *Spirit of St. Louis*, back to the United States on its transit home. The station ship *Scorpion*, at the end of several years of maintenance problems, was finally sent back to the United States for decommissioning as Rear Admiral Mark Bristol hauled down his pennant as commander of naval forces in the eastern Mediterranean, and gave up the position of the High Commissioner to Turkey.[85] Bristol was not done with the highest challenges of naval diplomacy and international affairs, however, as he was promoted to Admiral and took command of the Asiatic Fleet on 9 September 1927.[86]

In the Caribbean, tensions in Nicaragua, which began in 1926 over the approaching Presidential election, developed into a civil war. Ships of the Special Service Squadron, initially deployed to establish security along the coast the year before, spent the first half of 1927 actively operating on the Central American coast. In the closing weeks of 1926, American sailors and Marines landed at Bluefields to create a "neutral zone" for the protection of Americans and other foreign residents. The conflict spread across the east coast at first, and American landing parties went ashore at six different ports to create areas of safety by the end of the year. As 1927 began, the fighting shifted inland toward the capital at Managua and toward the more populated western provinces.[87]

Threats to American lives and property, as well as the international community, in Managua, resulted in a force of Marines and Sailors returning to the legation as a reinforced guard again. Initially, Marine deployments to the coast began as filler to cover the shipboard detachments who had moved ashore to set up the protected safe havens. The Second Battalion, 5th Regiment, embarked USS *Argonne* at Guantanamo where they had been training and were the first major unit to sail for Bluefields. A company was left at the port of Rama to maintain security, and the remainder of the battalion moved through the canal aboard Argonne and landed on the west coast at Corinto at the end of January. The Marines deployed ashore to protect the port and began moving inland toward Managua. In February, Marine Observation Squadron No. 1 and a rifle company arrived via USS *Melville* and USS *Altair,* and established overflight and reconnaissance operations that "were at once found to be of great value."[88]

The situation in Nicaragua continued to deteriorate and the remainder of the 5th Regiment of Marines and the command staff of the Second Brigade embarked USS *Henderson* and were delivered to Corinto. Brigadier General Logan Feland, in command of the Second Brigade, assumed overall command of the Nicaragua operations ashore. In April and May, negotiations began between the opposing groups, and an agreement was reached on 7 May. At that point, the Nicaraguans asked the Marines to assist in the enforcement of the cease-fire and the execution of the overall disarmament effort. The 11th Regiment was dispatched from Haiti and arrived within two weeks of the ceasefire. By the middle of June, the Marines began redeploying some of their forces, returning them either home or to their previous missions. By the end of the year, the 5th Regiment, light one battalion, was still in the country supported by one of the Marine aviation squadrons. In total, a Marine expeditionary force of 3,000 was transported to the Nicaraguan coast. They established safe havens on both coasts in ports where American businesses were located and established security in Managua and the route between the capital and the Corinto and then assumed responsibility for enforcing the disarmament agreement and establishing the Guardia Nacional de Nicaragua to maintain security.[89]

During the Nicaraguan mission, the Special Service Squadron rapidly ran out of resources and ships, and Navy headquarters dispatched ships from the rest of the fleet to support. At the beginning of 1927, five destroyers of the Scouting Fleet had been dispatched to join the Squadron, and by the end of January, two light cruisers also sailed into Nicaraguan waters. The seven ships of the Scouting Fleet remained as peace negotiations began between the warring sides and were relieved by Destroyer Squadron 12 of the Battle Fleet from the west coast.

During a year filled with the ongoing civil war in China, the instability in Nicaragua, and continued diplomatic missions in Europe and the Mediterranean, the Navy was overloaded with tasking. In addition to its international missions, the Navy responded to a widespread flooding event on the Mississippi River, which remains the most destructive river flood in American history. Beginning with heavy rainfall in late 1926, the tributaries of the Mississippi began overflowing their banks, and the water rushed across the region, affecting Missouri, Illinois, Kansas, Tennessee, Kentucky, Arkansas, Louisiana, Mississippi, Oklahoma, and Texas.[90] The Navy disaster relief efforts were based out of the Pensacola Naval Air Station, where operations continued from 16 April through 16 June 1927. These efforts included 32 aircraft flying search, rescue, and logistics missions, the USS *Allegheny* and USS *Bagaduce* operating from Vicksburg, Mississippi, and naval communications units establishing 19 expeditionary radio stations across the region to support relief efforts.[91]

With so many active missions around the world, Secretary of the Navy Curtis Wilbur noted the dramatic pace of operations in his report to the President and Congress for the year. Crisis response and forward presence missions demanded more ships than the Asiatic Fleet, European forces, and Special Services Squadron were able to provide. Ships were detached at different times from the Battle Fleet and the Scouting Fleet in order to support real-world operations, rather than simply focus on their training and readiness. Secretary Wilbur wrote that the demands of naval crisis response and presence "are seriously affecting the efficiency or the operations of the United States Fleet."[92] The demands of history, and the events of the world around them, were forcing the Navy to do more than just concentrate on preparing for war.

1928

After the demanding year of operations in 1927, the Navy began to redistribute its forces and reconsider some of its operations in 1928. The Secretary reported that the "conditions in China have improved considerably during the past year," but that many sailors and Marines remained in the Pacific theater providing the enhanced security initiated the previous year. The situation in Nicaragua had not improved as had been hoped when the Marines began assisting in the implementation of the disarmament agreement. With Marines active in combat in Nicaragua and large numbers still providing security in China, 950 Marines were removed from ship detachments with the Battle Fleet and were redistributed to forward-deployed forces. In addition to this, 270 sailors were detached from Battle Fleet ships to form a special force for duty in the administration of the coming 1928 election in Nicaragua. The Special Service Squadron continued supporting Nicaragua and other operations in the western hemisphere, while forces in European waters were significantly reduced.[93]

In China, the fighting along the Yangtze had calmed. *Guam*, the first of the new, purpose-designed river gunboats was launched from the Shanghai shipyards on 28 December 1927 and was joined by *Tutuila*, *Luzon*, *Mindanao*, *Panay*, and *Oahu* across 1928. These vessels allowed for a plan to strip down the old and decrepit *Elcano*, *Pampanya*, and *Villalobos* and strike them from the navy list.[94] The new gunboats on patrols from Hankou moved up river as far as Chongqing and monitored the American merchant traffic that was slowly returning to interior China. Missionaries and businesses, which had evacuated in 1927 to escape the unrest, began slowly returning to the interior as well.[95]

The Navy also reported the stabilization of the situation around Shanghai. One thousand Marines remained in the city maintaining security, while the majority of the fighting in the civil war had shifted north as the Nationalist forces pushed toward Beijing. While some Americans remained in the path of the advancing armies, the warlord Zhang Zuolin who had held Beijing and Tianjin withdrew his forces as the Nationalists advanced, and the area was spared from heavy fighting as the Nationalists took over.[96] Admiral Bristol watched the advance carefully, deploying his flagship (a cruiser), two light cruisers, 17 destroyers, 11 submarines, four tenders, four minesweepers, a transport, and an oiler into the waters of Northern China to monitor the advance and provide support as needed. In addition, the balance of Brigadier General Butler's 3,000 Marines of the Third Brigade remained primarily dispersed around Beijing and the barracks at Tianjin. By the summer of 1928, as stability settled in after the Nationalist capture of Beijing, Bristol and Butler decided to reduce the size of the Marine force in China,

900 Marines were sent back to the United States, and 13 aircraft and their support units were returned to Guam.[97]

At the time of the Navy Department's report to the President and Congress in 1927, there was optimism that the situation in Nicaragua was improving. The disarmament agreement brokered by American negotiator Henry Stimson and signed in May 1927 offered what appeared to be a path toward stability. The Marine Corps had begun reducing its force, focusing on training the Nicaraguan national guard that summer. Only 1,200 Marines and four ships assigned to the Special Service Squadron remained by the end of August. However, the agreement did not hold. Forces loyal to Augusto Sandino retained their arms and swung into action as a guerilla force against the Americans and their Nicaraguan hosts. By January 1928, Sandino and his followers had attacked several Nicaraguan towns and an American-owned mine, and it was determined that heavier Marine Corps forces needed to return to the country.[98]

After significant combat operations in the fall and autumn of 1927, naval intelligence estimated that Sandino's force had grown to 1,000 men, and it became clear that reinforcements were needed. Brigadier General Feland returned to Nicaragua in command of the Second Brigade, reinforced by an additional regiment of Marines. The 11th Regiment arrived from Norfolk, Virginia, aboard multiple navy ships between 15 and 20 January. The Marine aviation force was also reinforced, and air raids began against the town of El Chipote that had been captured by the Sandino rebels.[99]

This set a pattern for combat across the southern portion of Nicaragua through early 1928. Marine units fighting alongside Guardia Nacional assaulted Sandinista positions and patrolled the countryside, engaging in firefights and skirmishes. Marine Corps aviation units flew reconnaissance and bombing missions, and began developing the tactics of close air support. As patrols put pressure on the rebels, they moved around the country increasing their attacks in new regions as the Marines and Guardia pursued them. At the end of May, the Nicaraguan Government began an amnesty program for guerillas who turned in their arms and surrendered to government forces. Over the summer, more than 1,000 Nicaraguans turned themselves in, which the Marines reported as having "a great decrease in their activities."[100]

Fighting between 1927 and 1928 had pushed the date of the Nicaraguan Presidential election to November 1928. Army Brigadier General Frank McCoy was tasked with leading the electoral commission put together by the Americans to assist in the administration of the election. As the fighting slackened in the summer of 1928, the Marines continued to provide security, while detachments of Sailors were brought into the country to support the logistics behind the elections. By the time of the election, 5,000 Marines, 500 sailors and naval officers, and 21 aircraft were in Nicaragua to provide security and administer the election. A battalion of sailors was made up of detachments from the Battle Fleet and led by 29 Ensigns who had been explicitly selected for their Spanish language skills. Working for General McCoy, Marine Corps aviation flew many of these sailors and Marines across the country to staff polling stations and collect the ballots for their return to Managua for counting. Held on 4 November 1928, the election was held up as a success with Secretary Wilbur reporting the election as "satisfactory to a large majority of the Nicaraguan people, and without difficulty or disorder."[101]

Other needs for naval vessels continued across the world, even as demands on the fleet for operations in the Pacific and the Caribbean remained high through 1928. The cruisers *Cleveland*, *Denver*, and *Tulsa* each made diplomatic visits to Honduras through the summer to "foster friendly relations."[102] In addition, the USS *Hannibal* and *Nokomis* continued their survey and charting operations on the coast of Cuba, and Niagara worked on charting the Gulf of Panama.[103] However, with so many tasks for American naval ships, Naval Forces Europe saw a dramatic reduction in its size and missions. The former Constantinople station ship *Scorpion*, which had finally returned to the United States in 1927, was in such terrible condition that she was stricken from the Navy list in 1928. Early in the year, after only seven months in European waters, Destroyer Division 38 returned to the United States without relief. This left only the flagship of Naval Forces Europe, the cruiser *Detroit*, in the Mediterranean and northern European waters where the ship continued to work with the State Department and provide what support a single vessel was capable of providing.[104]

1929

Fleet Problem IX dominated the exercise and training of the Battle Fleet and Scouting Fleet in 1929. For the first time, each side in a Fleet Problem had its own aircraft carrier. The results of the exercise, and the operational analysis and debates following those results, had a significant impact on the doctrinal development to come and the continuing advancement of naval aviation.[105] While these activities were significant to the future of the Navy, the rest of the United States' naval forces remained actively employed far from the coast of Panama and continued on the myriad of tasks that had already come to demand their time across the 1920s.

The Asiatic Fleet remained busy in Chinese waters for much of 1929, but, by the end of the year, some of the forces in northern Chinese waters were able to redeploy back to the Philippines and make port calls in other parts of the western Pacific. Over the year, the American reports from the Asiatic Fleet were that the Nationalist government had been able to strengthen their position by unifying most of China and largely maintained security, which allowed for the withdrawal of a significant portion of both the navy ships and the Marine forces in China. The Yangtze Patrol Force continued its work, now with all six of the new gunboats. In January and February, there was tension in the vicinity of the Wusong forts north of Shanghai as local military authorities began detaining American merchant vessels. American naval vessels arrived to help resolve the issues. Ships responded to renewed tensions at Nanjing and on the Shandong peninsula, and Admiral Bristol ordered his ships to move between coastal port towns throughout the year in order to protect American interests and offer diplomatic signals to the Nationalist government. As a part of these diplomatic efforts, Bristol joined the American minister to China as an American representative at the funeral ceremonies for Chinese nationalist leader Sun Yat-sen.[106]

In late 1928, the cruiser *Pittsburgh*, Light Cruiser Division 2, and most of the fleet's destroyers had left northern Chinese waters. They returned to the Philippines via port calls in Guam and Japan. At the end of January 1929, they arrived back in the Manila area in time for two weeks of joint exercises with the Army in Philippine waters. Light Cruiser Division 2, which had been dispatched from the Battle Fleet to reinforce the Asiatic Fleet the previous year, was sent home mid-year, and *Trenton*, *Memphis*, and *Milwaukee* made port calls in Japan before returning to California. While the slowing of the demands on the Asiatic Fleet in northern Chinese waters reduced operational tempo and allowed the Battle Fleet to reclaim its cruisers, diplomatic and trade protection requirements on the southern coast and exercises with the Army continued to keep the Asiatic Fleet busy in a wide range of missions.[107]

The Marine Corps' operations in China also experienced a reduction in tempo in 1929. The year started with 4,000 Marines of the Third Brigade under General Butler in the country. By the end of the summer, most of the Third Brigade had been redeployed out of China, leaving the 4th Regiment with 1,200 Marines mostly in Shanghai.[108] A reinforced Legation Guard of 500 Marines also remained in Beijing, while Tianjin barracks had been emptied of Marines. By the end of the summer, the entire force at Tianjin had been withdrawn, 500 Marines remained in Beijing as the reinforced Legation Guard, and two battalions made up of 1,200 men remained for security in Shanghai. Marines continued to protect American neighborhoods and establish security checkpoints around the city, as well as protecting communications between different cities in China and collaborating with the rest of the international community.[109]

In the Caribbean, the Special Service Squadron continued primarily to support operations in Nicaragua and the Marine Corps mission there. General J.M. Moncada had won the November election that was administered largely by sailors and Marines, and he took office on 1 January 1929. In negotiations with Rear Admiral D.F. Sellers, the commander of the Special Service Squadron, Moncada and the Americans agreed to begin limiting American involvement in Nicaragua. For a year and a half, Marines had been training the Guardia Nacional, and they agreed to turn over the responsibility for internal security to them. A contingent of Marines and sailors would remain in Nicaragua, but their mission would be limited to the protection of Americans and American property, and the assistance of the international community. The Marines would collaborate with the Guardia on the "preservation of order" when needed, but the Marine reinforcement of local authority "could not be counted on for an indefinite time."[110]

American and Nicaraguan forces continued to make progress against the few remaining guerillas after the election and as President Moncada was sworn in. Augusto Sandino and several other rebel leaders left Nicaragua for exile, and the number of guerillas continued to decline and was estimated by the Americans to total between 150 and 200 men in the summer of 1929. This led the Commandant of the Marine Corps to report "Nicaragua has been pacified."[111] Marines remained an important part of the Guardia Nacional, serving as the officers and continuing to operate alongside Marine Corps units, and Colonel D.C. McDougal remained the "chief" of the Guardia. However, the completed election and successful security operations at the beginning of 1929 led to the American conclusion that they could begin withdrawing sailors and Marines. By the end of the summer, the force, which had totaled 5,673 Americans at the time of the election, totaled 3,094.[112]

Operations in the wider Caribbean were limited based on the needs of the mission in Nicaragua. The Marines' First Brigade remained in Haiti, and the most important shift reported by the Commandant was the change in organization from what had been the Gendarmerie d'Haiti to the Garde d'Haiti. The security organization shifted to an agreement that explicitly created the path toward replacing Americans serving as officers with Haitians. Commandant Neville reported optimism over the Garde's growing nonpartisan approach to changes in Haitian political leadership, something that he considered vital to the success of Haiti's future as the Marines began to consider the possibility of their departure from the island.[113] Navy ships continued other minor operations in the Caribbean as they were available. The cruiser *Denver* arrived in Havana in February to commemorate the 30th anniversary of the sinking of the USS *Maine*.[114] The USS *Hannibal* and *Nokomis* continued their multi-year scientific and survey missions on the coast of Cuba for the Hydrographic Office, and the *Niagara* continued its ongoing mission in the Gulf of Panama. In addition, USS *Galveston* conducted a survey of the Cronito Harbor and its approaches off Nicaragua as a part of ensuring the safety of operations there.[115]

During the year, ships were often detached from the Battle Fleet and Scouting Fleet for additional duty across 1929. In June, Battleship Division 2, made up of *Florida*, *Arkansas*, and *Utah*, was detached from the Scouting Fleet and embarked with Naval Academy midshipmen for a European summer cruise to Barcelona, Naples, Gibraltar, and Weymouth. The older battleships *New York* and *Wyoming* were detached from the Scouting Fleet to sail for Bermuda and then Havana, Cuba, as a part of the Naval Reserve Officers' Training Cruise for the NROTC units on the east coast. USS *Mississippi* detached from the Battle Fleet for the west coast NROTC cruise to Puget Sound and British Columbia.[116]

Even as demand for American naval forces was reduced in both China and Nicaragua, operational tempo remained high. The Battle Fleet and the Scouting Fleet routinely detached ships for other missions besides their primary goal of preparing the Navy for war. For the second year in a row, two-thirds of the entire Marine Corps were deployed either in expeditionary operations to China, Nicaragua, and Haiti or aboard naval vessels around the world.[117] As the 1920s came to a close, the need for forward-operating naval forces remained high despite the year's critical lessons from Fleet Problem IX and the continued development of doctrine and preparation for the potential for war.

Notes

1 "Report of the Secretary of the Navy," in *Annual Reports of the Department of the Navy, 1920* (Washington, DC: Government Printing Office, 1921), 3–5.
2 "Report of the Secretary," 1920, 6–8.
3 Ibid., 29–33.
4 Ibid., 33.
5 Gibson Bell Smith, "Guarding the Railroad, Taming the Cossacks: The U.S. Army in Russia, 1918–1920," *Prologue Magazine* 34, no. 4 (Winter 2022), www.archives.gov/publications/prologue/2002/winter/us-army-in-russia-2.html.
6 "Report of the Secretary," 1920, 34.
7 Naval History and Heritage Command, "South Dakota I," *Dictionary of American Naval Fighting Ships*, www.history.navy.mil/research/histories/ship-histories/danfs.html (henceforth DANFS.)
8 All Chinese place names have been rendered in accepted twenty-first century romanization rather than the inconsistent usage and spellings offered in the primary sources.
9 "Report of the Secretary," 1920, 34. Naval History and Heritage Command, "South Dakota I," DANFS. Tolley, *Yangtze Patrol*, 83–85.
10 Yerxa, *Admirals and Empire*, 81.
11 "Report of the Secretary," 1920, 35.
12 "Marine Corps, Report of the Major General Commandant," in *Annual Reports of the Department of the Navy, 1920* (Washington, DC: Government Printing Office, 1921), 1059–60.
13 "Report of the Secretary," 1920, 36.
14 Ibid., 36–38.

15 "Report of the Secretary of the Navy," in *Annual Reports of the Department of the Navy, 1921* (Washington, DC: Government Printing Office, 1922), 2–5.

16 "Report of the Chief of Naval Operations," in *Annual Reports of the Department of the Navy, 1921* (Washington, DC: Government Printing Office, 1922), 19.

17 "Report of the Secretary," 1921, 6.

18 Still, *Victory Without Peace*, 191–92.

19 Ibid., 209. "Report of the Secretary," 1921, 6.

20 "Report of the Secretary," 1921, 6–7. Naval History and Heritage Command, "South Dakota I," DANFS. Schurmann quoted in Tolley, *Yangtze Patrol*, 96.

21 Tolley, *Yangtze Patrol*, 97.

22 Ibid., 97–98.

23 Quoted in Ibid., 102.

24 "Report of the Secretary," 1921, 7.

25 Millett, "The State Department's Navy," 121–22.

26 "The Marine Corps," in *Annual Reports of the Department of the Navy, 1921* (Washington, DC: Government Printing Office, 1922), 52.

27 "Report of the Secretary of the Navy," in *Annual Reports of the Department of the Navy, 1922* (Washington, DC: Government Printing Office, 1923), 1.

28 David Armstrong, "China's Place in the New Pacific Order," in *The Washington Conference, 1921–22: Naval Rivalry, East Asian Stability, and the Road to Pearl Harbor*, ed. Erik Goldstein and John Maurer (New York: Routledge, 1994), 249–65.

29 "Report of the Chief of Naval Operations," in *Annual Reports of the Department of the Navy, 1922* (Washington, DC: Government Printing Office, 1923), 39–40.

30 "Report of the Secretary," 1922, 4.

31 Ibid., 5.

32 Ibid., 6.

33 "Marine Corps, Report of the Major General Commandant," in *Annual Reports of the Department of the Navy, 1922* (Washington, DC: Government Printing Office, 1923), 822.

34 "Report of the Secretary," 1922, 4.

35 Ibid., 5.

36 "Report of the Hydrographic Office," in *Annual Reports of the Department of the Navy, 1922* (Washington, DC: Government Printing Office, 1923), 136.

37 "Report of the Major General Commandant," 1922, 822.

38 "Report of the Bureau of Aeronautics," in *Annual Reports of the Department of the Navy, 1922* (Washington, DC: Government Printing Office, 1923), 409. "Report of the Surgeon General," in *Annual Reports of the Department of the Navy, 1922* (Washington, DC: Government Printing Office, 1923), 261.

39 "Report of the Secretary," 1922, 5.

40 "Report of the Secretary of the Navy," in *Annual Reports of the Department of the Navy, 1923* (Washington, DC: Government Printing Office, 1924), 3–6.

41 "Report of the Secretary," 1923, 7–8.

42 Ibid., 15–16. Tolley, *Yangtze Patrol*, 116–17. "Shanghai Foreigners Ask Action," *New York Times*, May 20, 1923, 3.

43 "America Speeds Ships and Food: Navy Vessels, Army Transports, and Merchant Craft Rushing Supplies to Japan," *New York Times*, September 6, 1923, 1. "Stewart II," *DANFS* (henceforth DANFS.)

44 "Report of the Secretary," 1923, 16.

45 Ibid., 17–18.

46 Ibid., 18.
47 Ibid., 20–21.
48 "Marine Corps, Report of the Major General Commandant," in *Annual Reports of the Department of the Navy, 1923* (Washington, DC: Government Printing Office, 1924), 969–70.
49 "Report of the Secretary of the Navy," in *Annual Reports of the Department of the Navy, 1924* (Washington, DC: Government Printing Office, 1925), 6–7. Tolley, *Yangtze Patrol*, 117.
50 "Report of the Secretary," 1924, 6–7. Braisted, *Diplomats in Blue*, 23–29.
51 "Report of the Secretary," 1924, 8–9.
52 Ibid., 9–10. Tim Merrill, *Honduras: A Country Study* (Washington, DC: General Printing Office, 1995), 26–27. "Honduras Factions Sign Peace Treaty," *New York Times*, May 6, 1924, 1.
53 "Report of the Secretary," 1924, 193–94.
54 "Marine Corps, Report of the Major General Commandant," in *Annual Reports of the Department of the Navy, 1924* (Washington, DC: Government Printing Office, 1925), 677–78.
55 "Report of the Chief of Naval Operations," in *Annual Reports of the Department of the Navy, 1925* (Washington, DC: Government Printing Office, 1926), 72, 74–75.
56 "Report of the Secretary of the Navy," in *Annual Reports of the Department of the Navy, 1925* (Washington, DC: Government Printing Office, 1926), 1.
57 "Report of the Secretary," 1925, 5.
58 Ibid., 6.
59 Cole, *Gunboats and Marines*, 50–53.
60 Braisted, *Diplomats in Blue*, 39–43. Cole, *Gunboats and Marines*, 54–57. "Rival Regimes Rule in Shanghai," *New York Times*, July 30, 1925, 11.
61 Cole, *Gunboats and Marines*, 59–61, 66. "Increase Defenses to Guard Shameen," *New York Times*, June 28, 1925, 21.
62 "Report of the Secretary," 1925, 7.
63 Ibid., 8–9.
64 Ibid., 30.
65 "Report of the CNO," 1925, 75.
66 "Report of the Secretary," 1925, 58–59.
67 "Report of the Secretary of the Navy," in *Annual Reports of the Department of the Navy, 1926* (Washington, DC: Government Printing Office, 1927), 5–6.
68 "Report of the Secretary," 1926, 6–7. Cole, *Gunboats and Marines*, 85–90. Braisted, *Diplomats in Blue*, 101–12.
69 "Report of the Chief of Naval Operations," in Annual *Reports of the Department of the Navy, 1926* (Washington, DC: Government Printing Office, 1927), 74.
70 "Report of the Secretary," 1926, 7.
71 "Report of the CNO," 1926, 66.
72 "Report of the Secretary," 1926, 7.
73 "Report of the Hydrographic Office," in *Annual Reports of the Department of the Navy, 1926* (Washington, DC: Government Printing Office, 1927), 186.
74 "Report of the Secretary," 1926, 8.
75 "Report of the Major General Commandant of the United States Marine Corps," in *Annual Reports of the Department of the Navy, 1925* (Washington, DC: Government Printing Office, 1926), 1233.
76 "Report of the Secretary," 1926, 8. "President Appeals for Relief Funds," *New York Times*, September 21, 1926, 1.
77 "Report of the Secretary," 1926, 9.

42 *"A Force for Peace"*

78 "Report of the Secretary of the Navy," in *Annual Reports of the Department of the Navy, 1927* (Washington, DC: Government Printing Office, 1928), 1.
79 "Report of the Secretary," 1927, 3–4.
80 Ibid., 3.
81 Ibid., 5–6. Braisted, *Diplomats in Blue*, 113–30.
82 "Report of the Secretary of the Navy," in *Annual Reports of the Department of the Navy, 1928* (Washington, DC: Government Printing Office, 1929), 5. In the 1928 report, the Secretary clarified and added to some of the reporting on events in China from 1927.
83 "Report of the Secretary," 1927, 6. Tolley, *Yangtze Patrol*, 165–67.
84 "Report of the Major General Commandant of the United States Marine Corps," in *Annual Reports of the Department of the Navy, 1927* (Washington, DC: Government Printing Office, 1928), 1193. Cole, *Gunboats and Marines*, 111–33.
85 "Report of the Secretary," 1927, 6–7.
86 Ibid., 3. Braisted, *Diplomats in Blue*, 166.
87 "Report of the Secretary," 1927, 7.
88 "Report of the Major General Commandant," 1927, 1192.
89 Ibid., 1193.
90 John M. Berry, "After the Deluge," *Smithsonian Magazine*, November 2005, www.smithsonianmag.com/history/after-the-deluge-111555373/.
91 "Report of the Secretary," 1927, 9.
92 Ibid., 10.
93 "Report of the Secretary," 1928, 1–4.
94 Ibid., 16.
95 Ibid., 4–5.
96 "Report of the Chief of Naval Operations," in *Annual Reports of the Department of the Navy, 1928* (Washington, DC: Government Printing Office, 1929), 95.
97 "Report of the Secretary," 1928, 5. Cole, *Gunboats and Marines*, 162.
98 "Report of the Secretary," 1928, 6–7.
99 "Report of the Major General Commandant of the United States Marine Corps," in *Annual Reports of the Department of the Navy, 1928* (Washington, DC: Government Printing Office, 1929), 1241. Wray R. Johnson, *Biplanes at War: US Marine Corps Aviation in the Small Wars Era, 1915–1934* (Lexington, KY: University Press of Kentucky, 2019), 220–22.
100 "Report of the Major General Commandant," 1928, 1242–43.
101 "Report of the Secretary," 1928, 7. Johnson, *Biplanes at War*, 230.
102 "Report of the Secretary," 1928, 6.
103 "Report of the Hydrographic Office," in *Annual Reports of the Department of the Navy, 1928* (Washington, DC: Government Printing Office, 1929), 235.
104 "Report of the Secretary," 1928, 6.
105 See Felker, *Testing American Sea Power* and Nofi, *To Train the Fleet for War*.
106 "Report of the Secretary of the Navy," in *Annual Reports of the Department of the Navy, 1929* (Washington, DC: Government Printing Office, 1930), 4–5. Braisted, *Diplomats in Blue*, 195–96.
107 "Report of the Chief of Naval Operations," in *Annual Reports of the Department of the Navy, 1929* (Washington, DC: Government Printing Office, 1930), 85–86.
108 "Report of the Major General Commandant of the United States Marine Corps," in *Annual Reports of the Department of the Navy, 1929* (Washington, DC: Government Printing Office, 1930), 1185.

109 "Report of the Major General Commandant," 1929, 1185. Edwin P. Hoyt, *The Lonely Ships: The Life and Death of the U.S. Asiatic Fleet* (New York: David McKay Company, 1976), 113.
110 "Report of the CNO," 1929, 88.
111 "Report of the Major General Commandant," 1929, 1184.
112 "Report of the CNO," 1929, 89.
113 "Report of the Major General Commandant," 1929, 1186.
114 "Report of the CNO," 1929, 87.
115 "Report of the Hydrographic Office," in *Annual Reports of the Department of the Navy, 1929* (Washington, DC: Government Printing Office, 1930), 203.
116 "Report of the CNO," 1929, 82–83.
117 "Report of the Major General Commandant," 1929, 1183.

II "The Prestige of Its Flag"
The U.S. Navy and Marine Corps of the 1930s

1930

The start of a new decade brought a rekindled hope of more arms limitation treaties, as the world's naval powers met in London in January. Secretary of the Navy Charles Adams sailed for London as one of the American delegates, again joining representatives from the United Kingdom, Japan, Italy, and France. In the aftermath of the failure at Geneva to produce any agreement several years earlier, the London negotiations resulted in a new treaty that regulated submarines, cruisers, and destroyers, all of which had been left out of the Five Power Pact signed in Washington. The most immediate result of the successful negotiation, as Secretary Adams brought the treaty back to Washington for ratification, was a reorganization of the U.S. Navy's fleet by placing nearly all submarines under their own command as part of The Control Force, creating a part of the fleet explicitly organized for administrative, doctrinal, and training missions, and the separation of the Carrier Divisions into their own aviation focused organization, removing them from the Battle Fleet or Scouting Fleet organization. Notably, in the reorganization of the navy, Naval Forces Europe disappeared from the naval organization, while the Asiatic Fleet and the Special Service Squadron remained. Yet, the overall missions of the Navy, as outlined by Secretary Adams, remained the same: exercise and train "in case of emergency," protect American interests abroad, assist allies and partners of the United States, and "cultivate friendly relations with foreign people."[1]

The American hope for stability in China at the end of the 1920s, which had come with the success of the Nationalists, was challenged in the events of 1930. For the first time, the Department of the Navy's report mentioned "so-called communistic activities" as a problem alongside banditry and civil war. From the American perspective, the Nationalist Army's efforts to mass in order to consolidate power left large areas of the country uncovered by security forces. Crime would rise in these areas, as would the potential for communist activity. The Secretary

DOI: 10.4324/9781003409670-3

reported that, as a result, "American lives and interests have been under continual hazard in widely separated areas."[2]

Admiral C.B. McVay Jr., who had taken command from Bristol and had previously served as Commander of the Yangtze Patrol Force, remained almost the entire year in Chinese waters aboard his flagship *Pittsburgh*. Destroyer Division 38 relieved Destroyer Division 45, which returned to the Battle Fleet on the west coast, but largely the forces in the western Pacific remained the same as the prior year. The rise in both bandit activity and the growing communist movement in China resulted in numerous instances of American naval forces, particularly the Yangtze Patrol, being fired on. At the end of 1929, USS *Tulsa* arrived at Hankou, upstream from Nanjing on the Yangtze, to evacuate Americans caught in the ongoing violence, and USS *Guam* went further up river to Yichang. In June, aggressive fighting resulted in the deployment of *Tulsa* and *Guam* again, this time in anticipation of their need in the vicinity of Changsha. Around the same time, local officials in Xiamen notified the American consul that increased fighting meant they could no longer protect Americans and other foreigners, and the destroyer *Barker* was dispatched to the coastal town on the Taiwan Strait.[3] The gunboats of the Yangtze Patrol Force continued their work along the river. Firing on American ships became so common that the force instituted a convoy system and sailed on escort duty as much as general patrolling to protect merchant traffic on the river. The Secretary reported that "notwithstanding these precautions, attacks upon convoys, escorts, and individual ships have been frequent, resulting in casualties to both naval personnel and the passengers and crews of merchant vessels."[4]

Colonel C.H. Lyman and the Fourth Marines remained stationed in Shanghai during 1930 after the departure of the Third Brigade at the end of the previous year. The regiment of 1,200 Marines had a relatively peaceful period; Commandant B.H. Fuller reported that they had "preserved cordial relations with the Chinese people and their officials." Lyman and his officers used relative quiet to build relationships both with the Chinese and with other international forces in the city. They instituted local marksmanship and drill competitions, as well as athletic and recreational activities together. Despite the "disturbed political conditions and resultant strife," the Marines had a quiet year.[5]

The Special Service Squadron remained active in the Caribbean in 1930, with most of its operations focused around support to the Marine Corps' Second Brigade in Nicaragua. In addition, ships from the squadron worked with the State Department making port calls in Latin America, supported the Commission for the Study and Review of Conditions in Haiti appointed by President Hoover,[6] and continued to support the work of the Hydrographic office with *Hannibal*, *Nokomis*, and *Niagara* conducting the ongoing survey operations. The approach of another Presidential election in Nicaragua in 1931 and the prior agreements established that the United States would administer the election as it had in 1928. President Herbert Hoover appointed Captain Alfred Johnson to lead the effort, and in 1930, the Nicaraguan Supreme Court appointed him Chair of the Board of Elections. Planning began well in advance, following the outline of the efforts from 1928. A naval battalion was assembled to support the election, with many of the same enlisted sailors and Marines who had administered polling places in the prior election still available, led by officers of the Navy, Marine Corps, and some Army officers who had accompanied Brigadier General McCoy during his leadership of the 1928 effort. In total, 300 sailors and 250 Marines were detailed for the election administration.[7]

The Second Brigade continued operations in Nicaragua, and the Marine Corps continued to train and lead the Nicaraguan Guardia Nacional. The first half of the year was relatively quiet, and Marine units focused on garrisons at Managua, Matagalpa, and Ocotal, with detachments deployed to areas where guerrilla or bandit activity required them.[8] Because of the relative stability, the Marine force was reduced in early 1930 and a second time as the summer approached. By the end of the summer, there were 965 Marines remaining in Nicaragua, with another 208 Marine officers serving with the Guardia Nacional, which remained under the command of Colonel McDougal. Following the reduction in forces, guerilla activity increased. However, according to the Marine reports, the Guardia was able to respond to the increased activity with little need for support from American units other than continuing air support from Marine Corps aviation.[9] It was reported that summer that Augusto Sandino had returned from exile, but there was no noticeable change in activity, and the estimated strength of the guerilla forces was reported as 300 men, much lower than at the height of Sandino's prior campaign.[10]

As the economic challenges of the Great Depression spread beyond the developed countries of the world, both Nicaragua and Haiti began to see the impact. The Navy Department's report for 1930 explained that Nicaragua "has not escaped a share in the world-wide economic depression, and this condition has apparently contributed to the prevalence of banditry." However, the increasing political security and the reduction in theft and protection money being paid to bandit or guerilla bands appeared to balance the impact of the depression on the coffee industry, which dominated Nicaragua's economy.[11] Haiti was not as lucky, however. The Secretary reported that political opposition movements "coupled with economic depression, brought about a state of unrest which for a time threatened the internal peace of Haiti." The resulting labor strikes and spreading disaffection resulted in the reestablishment of martial law.[12]

The First Brigade, stationed in Haiti, had become what Commandant Fuller described as "largely a skeletonized unit."[13] The rising political unrest that spread across the country in late 1929 and 1930 overcame the largely quiet and secure situation, which had predominated for a decade and sparked President Hoover's effort to establish the commission to see if the occupation could be ended. Strikes in Port au Prince and Cap Haitien remained relatively peaceful and within the capabilities of the Haitian Garde. However, things degenerated in Aux Cayes when, in December 1929, a Marine patrol collaborating with a local Garde d'Haiti unit was surrounded at sunset by a group of an estimated 1,000 protesters. Marine reports characterized them as "male rioters bent upon overcoming the police and looting the town." According to the Marine reports, after attempting to fire warning shots and receiving direct physical attacks by the rioters, the Marines opened fire on the crowd "in self-defense." The crowd dispersed quickly, and several Haitians were killed in the exchange. Commandant Fuller reported that "order had been restored throughout the Republic" by the start of 1930. By February 1930, when the Commission arrived to begin their discussions with the Haitian government, the overt tensions had largely passed.[14]

At the start of September 1930, a massive hurricane swung through the eastern Caribbean, causing significant damage to Santo Domingo. Initial estimates by the American government were that 2,700 were killed, 8,000 were injured, and property damage was roughly 25 million dollars. The Navy immediately responded by sending USS *Grebe* with aid from the U.S. Virgin Islands, as well as medical professionals from the occupation forces in Haiti.[15] As aid began to flow, other parts of the Navy Department also swung into action. Aviation units from Haiti and the United States began flying relief supplies to overcome continuing challenges of opening the port facilities. The destroyer USS *Gilmer* was loaded with medical and relief supplies from the Navy and departed for Santo Domingo with Major Thomas Watson on board, who President Trujillo appointed as the government food and relief administrator.[16] After two weeks of around-the-clock work by naval forces in the country, the American Red Cross Relief Committee took over responsibility for the ongoing relief efforts.[17]

1931

A year into the terms of the London Naval Treaty, the United States was in the depths of the Great Depression. Rather than building the fleet to the limits of the treaty, the Navy began cutting its expenditures. Between 1930 and 1932, the Navy reduced the number of ships in full commission, reduced the number of sailors in the crews of the ships that were left, reduced the number of Marines in the Corps, cut back on the building programs for new ships, and cut back on the alterations or repair of ships.[18] In compliance with President Hoover's approach to handling the depression, the Navy Department made several rounds of budget cuts across the 1931 fiscal year. The Hoover administration used the London Treaty as an opportunity to squeeze more savings from the Navy. Six destroyer squadrons were cut, 16 ships decommissioned, eight moved into reserve status, and 25 submarines were removed from active commission.[19] Projects were cut, repairs deferred, and expenditures pushed to the plans for the next fiscal year.[20] With the reductions in the budget of the American fleet, the demands of forward operations remained in 1931. Missions of the Asiatic Fleet continued in Chinese waters, and the Special Service Squadron remained active in Nicaraguan waters and the wider Caribbean.

The Asiatic Fleet remained under the command of Admiral McVay, first aboard *Pittsburgh* as his flagship, followed by the newly commissioned heavy cruiser *Houston* when it arrived late in February. Before returning to the United States, *Pittsburgh* embarked Dwight F. Davis, the serving Governor General of the Philippines, for a two-week diplomatic cruise of western Pacific nations. *Pittsburgh* sailed for the United States via the Suez Canal and diplomatic port calls in the Mediterranean before it reached Norfolk in June and was almost immediately decommissioned as another cost-saving mechanism. Also sent home from the Asiatic Fleet and decommissioned were the minesweepers *Hart* and *Rizal*. However, the force remained relatively large and busy with 53 total ships, including *Houston*, 19 destroyers, 12 submarines, ten gunboats, and many tenders and support vessels.[21]

Several diplomatic cruises were made through the ports of southern China and other nations in the region. Destroyer squadrons rotated between presence missions in northern Chinese waters and the Manila area, while the ships of the South China Patrol Force and the gunboats of the Yangtze Patrol Force continued their ongoing presence patrols and protection of American interests. The Navy Department's report lumped threatening events into a single "communist-bandit activities" label but stated that the efforts by Chiang Kai-shek to consolidate power resulted in "better prospects for peace and unity than at any time during the past ten years."[22]

However, by the middle of the year, tensions had returned. As the summer began, a division of destroyers was moved into Chinese waters to reinforce operations on the lower Yangtze and the three southernmost ports, allowing gunboats to focus up river. In early July, the gunboat USS *Guam* launched a rescue operation to save two missionaries "from communists" and came under fire near Yueyang, resulting in the death of a sailor while taking small arms fire from the shore. At the end of July, Communist forces attacked Changsha in Hunan province and USS *Palos* joined naval vessels from the British, Italians, and Japanese to help evacuate foreigners. Reports of communist activities growing in Fujian province resulted in the deployment of USS *Pillsbury* to Fuzhou to show the flag and protect American lives.[23] The summer also brought some of the worst flooding that central China had seen in a generation, with over 34,000 square miles of land in the Yangtze watershed flooded. Estimates were that 150,000 Chinese perished and the property damage was nearly $500 million dollars. Both divisions of Asiatic Fleet destroyers in addition to the *Houston* arrived and worked with consular officials in Hankou and Nanjing to evacuate Americans and assist the local governments with relief efforts.[24]

The start of the summer also saw new and destabilizing developments on the South China coast, as a group of leaders established a new "National Government of China" and claimed Guangzhou as their capital. Reports reached the Asiatic Fleet that this new government mined some of the waters in the vicinity of Guangzhou and Swatow, and had gathered approximately 50,000 troops in control of Kwantung and Kwangsi provinces. The Chief of Naval Operations reported that "it would appear that China faces a continuing period of unsettled conditions."[25] Admiral McVay turned over command to Montgomery Taylor in September and assumed responsibility for these new challenges and the Japanese intervention in Manchuria, which began at the end of the year.

The Special Service Squadron remained active on the coast of Central America throughout 1931. Following the pattern of small reductions experienced by the Asiatic Fleet, the cruiser *Denver* was detached from the squadron in late 1930 and returned to Philadelphia where she was decommissioned in February. This followed on the heels of the decommissioning of *Galveston*, another long-time Special Service Squadron ship, in late 1930. In 1931, the squadron was made up of only three ships on permanent assignment, *Rochester*, *Sacramento*, and *Asheville*. Despite the reduction in force, the squadron encountered both ongoing operations and several new crises requiring a response.[26]

Guerilla activities continued in Nicaragua during 1931, and their operations shifted toward the east, which had remained relatively untouched by the unrest in previous years. Moving from their focus in the south and the central parts of the country caused the Special Service Squadron and Marines to shift their operations as well. *Rochester*, *Sacramento*, and *Ashville* all moved through the Panama Canal to the Caribbean side and took up positions in ports on the east coast. With violence rising, as "a precautionary measure," the aircraft carrier *Langley*, cruiser *Memphis*, and destroyers *Dupont* and *Schenck* were detached from the Scouting Force[27] following Fleet Problem XII in the Caribbean and arrived in the vicinity of Puerto Cabezas in mid-April to provide wider support. The reinforcements remained in Nicaraguan waters for a month, providing security for the evacuation of Americans and international business interests.[28]

The Marine units in Nicaragua continued their ongoing reductions and had largely concentrated in the vicinity of Managua. By the summer of 1931, there were 540 Marines in the Second Brigade, and another 209 officers and men serving with the Guardia Nacional of Nicaragua, and further reductions were planned to bring the force down to 225 Marines by the end of the year. The plan was for a complete withdrawal in 1932. Support continued for the Guardia Nacional, but the number of Nicaraguans commissioned into its officer ranks was increasing, and the Commandant reported optimism that Guardia operations could be turned entirely over to the Nicaraguans in the near future. Despite the confidence, violence continued, and other challenges presented themselves.

At the end of March, an earthquake rocked Managua, which caused the outbreak of a massive fire that burned 32 city blocks. The estimated death toll was over a thousand. At the request of the Nicaraguan government, Marines began enforcing a declaration of martial law and furnished guards and patrols throughout the city. Navy medical personnel set up aid stations and began providing medical assistance to the many injured. The Guardia quickly reconstituted itself and took over security responsibilities from the Marines. The Marines shifted to relief work. The USS *Lexington* was dispatched to Nicaraguan waters briefly, and its aircraft participated in the movement of relief supplies inland and the transport of more navy medical personnel. The hospital ship *Relief* was also dispatched to Corinto on the west coast, where she landed supplies and support.[29]

In the immediate aftermath of the earthquake, as the Marines focused on their relief efforts, Augusto Sandino's reconstituted guerilla force launched their new campaign in the east. Minor attacks occurred in the central provinces of Matagalpa and Nueva Segovia. The largest attack in the east was on Logtown, which was carried out while the local Guardia unit was away on a patrol. Marine Corps aircraft conducted attacks on the guerillas as they assaulted the town, and returning Guardia and Marine patrols fought them back out of town. One Marine officer was killed in the fighting, but so was Pedro Blandon, one of Sandino's closest aides and the commander of the attack.[30] Another minor attack occurred at the undefended town of Cabo Gracias a Dios where the local radio station was destroyed. As the Guardia collapsed on the fighting around Logtown, other coastal towns, such as Bluefields, were left undefended. The ships of the Special Service squadron organized landing parties of their sailors and their embarked Marines who went ashore. *Memphis* and *Ashville* established security in Puerto Cabezas and *Sacramento's* Marine detachment landed to do the same at Bluefields. By the end of April, the Guardia had returned, and the Americans embarked their ships.[31]

Just as the fighting in the eastern part of Nicaragua was underway, a revolt broke out in northern Honduras following unrest that the Chief

of Naval Operations attributed to "unemployment, unsatisfactory economic conditions and fostered by communistic propaganda."[32] The
revolutionaries occupied the city of Progresso but were pushed out by
government forces in a counter attack. With 1200 Americans, as well as
other international merchant interests, in the north of the country, the
State Department turned to the Navy. With the Special Service squadron conducting their landing operations on the east coast of Nicaragua,
the Navy decided that they "could not be spared," and ships from the
Scouting Force were rerouted to the area. *Memphis*, which had already
arrived in Nicaraguan waters following Fleet Problem XII, was rerouted
to Honduras and arrived at Puerto Castilla on 20 April. The cruisers
Marblehead and *Trenton* arrived at other ports soon after, and they were
joined by *Rochester* from the Special Service Squadron by the end of the
month once its operations in Nicaraguan waters were complete. Fighting continued, and former Honduran Minister of War General Gregorio
Ferrera arose as the leader of the revolt. His forces withdrew inland
and to the south, allowing for security to return to the coastal towns
of the north where American interests were concentrated. In May, the
Navy determined that it was safe to reduce forces, and *Rochester*, *Trenton*, and *Memphis* were redeployed, leaving *Marblehead* on the coast.
A rotation was continued for the remainder of the year, with *Marblehead* relieved by *Richmond*, which was followed by *Sacramento*.

As the year came to a close, naval presence and crisis response continued to be an active part of the U.S. Navy's missions around the world.
Ten ships were commissioned and joined the fleet throughout the year.
However, with 62 ships placed out of commission during the year and
an additional 111 ships stricken from the Navy List, it was becoming
harder and harder for the Navy to maintain readiness and keep their
forces forward.[33] This was illustrated by the repeated use of Battle Force
and Scouting Force ships on missions for the Asiatic Fleet and the Special Services Squadron, a pattern that had been developing as the Navy
wrestled with the Hoover administration's cost-cutting response to the
Great Depression.

1932

Reductions to the Navy's budget continued in the final year of the Hoover Administration, with Secretary of the Navy Adams attempting to
sound the alarm in his annual report to the President and Congress. In
the early pages of his report, he clearly outlined the continued reductions
in both the appropriations for the Department and the expenditures,
and then stated clearly that "curtailment of expenditures has been made
principally at the expense of the fighting fleet." The reductions had five
results: the continued reduction in the number of ships in commission,

the reduction of the number of sailors on those ships, the reduction of the manpower of the Marine Corps, the curtailment of new building programs, and the curtailment of repairs and alterations to existing ships.[34]

In order to demonstrate that the budget cuts were more than theoretical reductions in American naval power, the Secretary outlined the force in comparison to the United Kingdom and Japan, the other major naval powers and signatories of the London Naval Treaty. When examining battleships, the Japanese were limited to ten ships and had all ten commissioned and fully manned; the British were limited to 15 and had 14 in full commission; and the Americans were limited to 15 and had 11 in full commission. In comparing aircraft carriers, the Japanese were authorized four, and they had four in commission and fully manned; the Royal Navy was authorized six, and they had three in full commission and three operating in reserve status; and the United States was authorized six and had only three. The Japanese had 12 heavy cruisers in commission, the British had 17 in commission, and the Americans had eight. The Japanese had 20 light cruisers in commission, the Royal Navy had 25 in full commission and eight in reserve, and the United States had ten light cruisers.[35] The numbers themselves spoke volumes. However, despite the continuing reductions in the size of the American Navy and its weakness compared to the other major naval powers, demands on American forward presence and crisis response did not diminish in 1932.

In assessing the work of forward-deployed naval forces in 1932, Chief of Naval Operations William Pratt wrote that the "Asiatic Fleet has had one of the busiest years on record."[36] In order to add more flexibility to the deployment models in the western Pacific, the destroyers of the Asiatic Fleet were reorganized from two divisions with six ships each to three divisions made up of four ships each. This allowed for the rotation of one of the divisions back to the United States in a further cost-cutting effort, and the ships were assigned to the Rotating-Reserve squadron that had been established at Mare Island. The remaining two destroyer divisions rotated between Manila's environs and operations along the Chinese coast. Pratt continued to report that, by the end of 1932, the American assessment was that China was "more completely disorganized than at any time since the Revolution of 1911." One government claimed and controlled Nanjing and its surrounding areas, the Japanese had intervened in Manchuria, the region was "uncertain," the newly established South China government in Guangzhou kept the area "estranged," and the continued recovery from flooding and the civil war placed a massive strain on security.[37]

In the waters at Tianjin, the Asiatic Fleet maintained a permanent presence first with the gunboat *Tulsa* followed by *Asheville* when it arrived in the western Pacific, reassigned from the Special Service Squadron. The reinforced Legation Guard of 475 Marines remained in Beijing, protecting the consulate and the international community there, though the Nationalist government in Beijing maintained well-established security during the year. With Yangtze River communities still recovering from the floods of the prior year and banditry rising, three destroyers were kept in constant rotation with the six gunboats of the Yangtze Patrol Force on the river.[38] In December 1931, Ms. Marie Halverstadt, an American missionary, was kidnapped and held for ransom. The destroyer USS *Stewart* was a Fuzhou and its officers assisted in the negotiations for the woman's release, which occurred by the end of January. In January, the master of one of the American-owned ships from the Yangtze Rapid Steamship Company was also kidnapped and held for ransom until 1 June when he was finally ransomed by the company. This followed on the heels of the murder of an American missionary in late 1931, while the Reverend Burton Nelson remained a hostage after his kidnapping in 1930.[39]

Northern China and the Yangtze, however, were not the only areas in need of American naval presence to help deal with crises. From April to June, communist activity in the area of Xiamen increased, and concerns for the safety of the International Settlement on Gulangyu rose in importance. The gunboats *Tulsa*, having been relieved at Tianjin by *Asheville*, *Sacramento*, recently arrived from its reassignment from the Special Service Squadron, and the submarine tender *Canopus* were dispatched to the waters around Xiamen. Meanwhile, the South China Patrol Force continued its operations in the vicinity of Guangzhou monitoring the new government there. Growing tensions between the Nanjing government and the Guangzhou government raised concerns for the Americans. While there seemed to be little relief in the tensions, *Tulsa* and *Canopus* sailed from Xiamen for other operations, leaving *Sacramento* on station for the remainder of the year.[40]

The year 1932 also introduced the first full year of the Japanese intervention in China. After the Mukden incident in Manchuria the previous autumn, tensions rose in the vicinity of Shanghai in January. The Fourth Marine Regiment remained stationed in Shanghai with 1,247 Marines, and another 400 Marines were sent from Manila in early February to reinforce the International Settlement. By February, the tensions had turned to open combat. The Japanese, having sent a group of ultranationalist Buddhist Monks into Shanghai to spark tensions and challenges to the safety of Japanese citizens in the city, deployed their Navy and Army to the city, and fighting broke out between the Chinese and the Japanese. The Marines executed "Plan A" for the defense of the International Settlement, establishing a perimeter and checkpoints and bringing a company of Chinese volunteers of the Shanghai Volunteer Corps serving as translators and guides into their units. As the fighting sharpened, the Marines created a second defensive line and increased their patrolling.[41]

"Stray" rounds from artillery duels between the Chinese defenders and the Japanese fell inside the perimeter nearly 100 times across the next two months, causing several close calls but no injuries to Marines. The Fleet flagship USS *Houston* arrived in Shanghai Harbor on 4 February and delivered eight officers and 326 enlisted to join the defenses. On 11 February, a Japanese bomber flew over the International Settlement and dropped a pair of bombs, which destroyed a cotton mill inside the Marine lines, killed six Chinese, and injured 15. Fighting between the Chinese and Japanese continued to place pressure in the area defended by the Marines until 4 March when Chinese forces abandoned the neighborhoods opposite the International Settlement, and the Japanese Army moved in to occupy the area. Slowly, the fighting tapered off. The 4th Marines continued their patrols and began to reduce their forces kept on the defensive perimeter. By mid-June, the International Settlement elected to rescind their "state of emergency" declaration from January, and the defensive positions were stood down as the Marines returned to their garrison positions.[42]

As tensions in Asia boiled over, and the U.S. Navy responded to the Chinese Civil War expanding into a war with the Japanese empire, forward presence operations continued in the Caribbean as well. The First Marine Brigade remained garrisoned in Haiti, with a total of 660 Marines, another 114 Marines serving in aviation squadrons assigned to the mission, and 105 Marines serving in leadership roles in the Garde d'Haiti. The Commandant reported a quiet year, where "mutual respect and consideration" between the Haitians and the Americans remained the rule, concluding that "there were no military operations during the year."[43]

Operations also continued in Nicaragua, where the Guardia Nacional proceeded to take over more and more of the security responsibilities, and more Nicaraguan officers assumed leadership roles. The Second Marine Brigade was located in Managua and had 500 Marines assigned. In addition, in Nicaragua, 180 Marines were serving in leadership positions in the Guardia Nacional, and there were 244 Marines assigned to aviation units in the country. Support to the Guardia was their primary mission, and the ground forces conducted "no operations in the field" during 1932. The Marines in Managua focused on training missions, helping develop the Guardia with small arms practice, patrol and "bush warfare" training, and preparing for security support to democratic elections. Plans were put in place to begin the withdrawal of the Second Marine Brigade from Nicaragua in late 1932 and 1933.

Despite the relative lack of ground operations, Marine Corps aviation made significant contributions to the effective operations of the Nicaraguan security forces. Throughout the year, Marine Corps aviation units flew reconnaissance missions, transport and resupply, photographic intelligence collection, and air attacks on known guerilla and bandit camps. In supporting roles, they also flew mapping missions, delivered mail to hard-to-reach northern communities, and supported the 1932 election mission, moving electoral observers and administrators and their supplies around the country.[44]

At the end of the year, Commandant Fuller pointed out the continued strain that forward presence and crisis response operations were placing on the Marine Corps, which had experienced a 15 percent reduction in its size in the past year. He wrote that the combination of demands and reduced resources "made it impossible for the corps [sic] to carry out its primary mission of supporting the United States Fleet by maintaining a force in readiness to operate with the fleet." He went on to assert that "the Marine Corps is not prepared to perform its allotted task in the event of a national emergency."[45] These warnings, when paired with the Secretary of the Navy's efforts in his report to Congress to demonstrate the relative decline of the U.S. Navy, in comparison with the British and Japanese, suggested that it would have made sense to consolidate the Battle Fleet in preparation for war. However, instead, the Navy and Marine Corps continued with their necessary forward presence and crisis response missions, with forward-deployed units often reduced in size but still needed for the wider protection of American interests.

1933

The start of the Franklin Roosevelt Administration brought changes to the way the U.S. government was approaching both the Great Depression and the Department of the Navy. Charles Adams completed his term in March 1933 when Claude Swanson was sworn in as the new Secretary of the Navy. With the passage of the National Industrial Recovery Act (NIRA), American shipyards came into focus as a source of both potential employment and producers of tangible goods that would benefit the American government and the American people. As a result, new naval construction found a new source of funding and support, and the Roosevelt Administration announced the construction of 32 new naval vessels, supported by the NIRA. As the Secretary reported, the building program would "prevent further weakening of our naval strength," and at the same time, "approximately 85% of the money spent on this naval construction will go directly into the pockets of labor . . . Every state will benefit."[46]

Between assuming his duties as Secretary in March and May, Secretary Swanson initiated an official review of American naval policy. A formal naval policy document was created and released to the public, providing overarching guidance for the development and missions of the Navy across the term of the new President. Largely, the missions of the

Navy and Marine Corps did not change. As they had been in previous annual reports from Secretaries under Herbert Hoover and Calvin Coolidge, the Navy would exercise and train to be prepared for a national emergency (a war), protect American interests in "disturbed areas," cooperate fully with other elements of the American government, and "cultivate friendly relations with foreign peoples."[47] The one minor deviation from prior expressions of the missions was the more expansive wording of cooperating with "other departments of the Federal Government" as opposed to just listing the State Department, perhaps an indication of what 21st-century strategists would call a "whole of government" view. The newly announced "United States Naval Policy" retained key forward presence and crisis response missions in the overall "General Naval Policy" statement and formally continued support for the Asiatic Fleet "and other such independent forces," as well as continuing hydrographic and scientific efforts of the department.[48]

The U.S. Fleet, with the Battle Force and Scouting Force remaining the main elements, continued to exercise and conduct the Fleet Problems throughout 1933. An earthquake struck California centered just offshore of Huntington Beach and Long Beach on 10 March, with 120 casualties and over $50 million in damage. The sailors of the Battle Force provided support to local authorities and aid efforts. Sailors manned neighborhood aid stations providing food and water to residents, and others aided the local police departments in patrols to maintain order.[49]

The Asiatic Fleet remained deployed to the western Pacific, and the Yangtze Patrol Force and South China Patrol Force continued their forward presence missions. Despite the reductions of the prior years, there was no reported reduction in the size of the force in 1933 as the ships remained in high demand throughout the theater. On the Yangtze, American gunboats continued to take fire from the shore as "roving bands of former soldiers and bandits" were active throughout the central portions of the country. The gunboats continued the policy of convoy operations with merchant vessels along the rivers, occasionally reinforced by destroyers. Fighting between Japanese and Chinese forces remained largely contained to the north, and as an inland problem, which resulted in less need for American naval monitoring. In the late summer, a truce was briefly negotiated at Tangku, which the Americans hoped would hold. In port towns and major cities, the Chinese population carried out widespread demonstrations against the Japanese intervention, as well as boycotts of Japanese business interests. They often raised tensions and the threat of violence against international communities, and American naval forces responded repeatedly throughout the year to help provide stability. The reinforced Legation Guard, now at about 540 Marines, continued their deployment in Beijing throughout 1933. Command of the Fleet transferred from Admiral Taylor to Frank Upham in August.[50]

The Special Service Squadron, which had been reduced to just three ships by the end of 1932, remained active throughout the Caribbean. The Navy and Marine Corps again supported the Nicaraguan Presidential election in late 1932. Admiral C.H. Woodward was appointed to head the Nicaraguan National Board of Elections by the Nicaraguan Supreme Court. Following the pattern of the efforts in prior years, the election was considered a success, and the new President Juan Sacasa was sworn in on 1 January 1933 in a peaceful transfer of power. The Marine Corps continued to support the Guardia Nacional, and Nicaraguan officers continued to replace the Americans in leadership positions. At the end of 1932, efforts began to eliminate American involvement entirely, and by January 1933, the Navy Department began executing the total withdrawal of naval forces from Nicaragua. The main body of the Fifth Regiment, the remaining Marine Corps unit, embarked USS *Henderson* and *Antares*, and sailed from Corinto once the new President was sworn in. The Nicaraguan intervention came to an end.[51]

Marine Corps operations in Haiti were likewise moving toward a conclusion. The First Brigade, with a total of around 900 Marines and sailors, remained garrisoned in Port au Prince and Cap Haitien. Marines continued to lead elements of the Garde d'Haiti, but, like in Nicaragua, the Haitian officers were slowly taking over the leadership positions. The Department reported to Congress that "conditions have been quiet, and the brigade has performed routine" duties throughout the year.[52]

With the withdrawal of Marines from Nicaragua, a brief truce negotiated between Chinese forces and the Japanese invasion forces in Manchuria, and quiet in Haiti, the first year of the Roosevelt Administration had seen reducing demand for naval forward presence. Despite the apparent overall respite, the new Secretary of the Navy kept forward presence and crisis response as key elements of the Navy's mission and naval policy. As 1934 would demonstrate, world events had a way of decreasing demands on naval forces, followed by increases depending on the contingency of history.

1934

The second year of the Roosevelt Administration brought with it continued good news for the Navy and Marine Corps, as the uniformed leadership continued to consider the overall state and size of the American naval forces. Congress passed the Vinson-Trammell Act that authorized a significant increase in shipbuilding and an effort to bring the U.S. Navy up to the limits of the London Naval Treaty. When combined with President Roosevelt's use of the NIRA and also the Emergency Employment Act, additional 24 naval vessels were put under construction between the fiscal year 1934 and fiscal year 1935, bringing the total to 70 ships under active construction. Those additions to the Fleet would still leave the overall force 78 vessels short of the authorized limit, and Secretary Swanson continued the pattern which had started with Secretary Adams laying out the British and Japanese naval force structure as a comparison. The momentum continued as the new ships were built, however, with eight ships commissioned and 30 older ships decommissioned in 1934. The only major change in organization was the creation of the Fleet Marine Force, and an effort to address Headquarters Marine Corps' continuing concerns that forward expeditionary operations and crisis response was overwhelming their ability to conduct fleet support missions.[53]

The Asiatic Fleet "performed their normal functions" in 1934 with the South China Patrol and the Yangtze Patrol continuing operations. The Yangtze gunboats continued convoy operations along the river in support of American and international merchants. Largely the conflict between the Japanese and the Chinese remained contained in Manchuria, which left the Asiatic Fleet little to do besides monitor the situation. The political dynamics of the competing warlords and governments in the south and southeast of China also generally did not change, leaving the officers of the Asiatic Fleet with a relatively stable, even if still dangerous, environment in which to operate in 1934. In June, an American destroyer joined by a minesweeper assisted the Royal Navy near the mouth of the Yellow River in a counterpiracy operation that rescued foreign passengers from a riverboat who had been taken hostage.[54]

The British also came to American assistance off of Hong Kong when a fire broke out aboard the submarine tender *Fulton*, participating in the South China Patrol. Being one of the oldest ships of the Asiatic Fleet, built in 1914, on 14 March, her amidships diesel engine caught fire. The fire spread quickly, and the crew was unable to control it. Gathering at the bow and the stern, the majority of the crew was taken off the ship by the destroyer HMS *Wishart* and the British merchant ship SS *Tsinan*. No one was injured, and a salvage crew was able to eventually put out the fire. Fulton was towed into Hong Kong, and later to Cavite, where she was deemed unsalvageable and decommissioned at the American naval base.[55]

The Marine units in China remained at their stations and remained about the same size as the previous few years. The Fourth Marine Regiment continued to protect the international community in Shanghai, continuing to keep an eye on the Japanese in the city but with no activity reported. The reinforced legation guard also remained in Beijing, which was similarly quiet.[56]

The Marines' other large deployment at the start of 1934 was the continuing occupation of Haiti by the First Marine Brigade. However, that mission was also coming to an end. The Marines had all been gathered in their garrisons at the two major cities, Port au Prince and Cap Haitien, and conducted no operations in 1934, instead experiencing what was reported as "a tranquil condition." The final efforts at "Hatianization" of the Garde d'Haiti were underway, with only 32 Marines left in any positions with the local security force at the start of the summer. President Roosevelt made a visit to Cap Haitien in July to reaffirm the agreement made the previous year to disengage in Haiti and finalize the transfer of all authority back to Haitian President Stenio Vincent. By August, the Marines' mission in Haiti was deemed complete, and the withdrawal of the remaining 750 men began for their return to the United States.[57]

The end of the intervention and occupation in Haiti while in keeping with the Roosevelt Administration's announced "Good Neighbor Policy" was not the end of American naval operations in the Caribbean. Unrest in Cuba had begun to draw the attention of the Special Service Squadron in late 1933, as several Cuban factions responded to the brutality and antidemocratic efforts of Gerardo Machado to maintain power. Rear Admiral C.S. Freeman, in command of the squadron, took his flagship *Richmond* to Havana harbor to signal American concern. The other two ships of the squadron also sailed for Cuban waters, and the force was reinforced with several destroyers, four Coast Guard cutters, and eight Coast Guard destroyers, which began patrolling Cuban waters. The battleship *Wyoming* embarked a battalion of Marines at Guantanamo Bay and also sailed for the north coast of the island in order to be ready to land at Havana. The political developments in Cuba resulted in the overthrow of Machado, which the American government seemed unconcerned with under the Good Neighbor policy. While the American naval forces remained offshore a new power struggle played out in Cuba, the Army officer Colonel Fulgencio Batista helped install Carlos Mendieta as the new President after six months of uprisings and counterrevolutions. The ships reinforcing the Special Service Squadron were slowly reassigned over the intervening months, but tensions remained elevated. By the summer, the battalion of Marines had returned to Guantanamo Bay but remained on alert, and another battalion remained in Florida in case it was needed. The three ships of the squadron remained nearby, reinforced with an additional light cruiser and two destroyers operating out of Guantanamo.[58]

Forward naval operations in the western Pacific, as well as ongoing crisis response missions in the Caribbean, kept the need for the Navy and Marine Corps' presence on the front pages of American newspapers in 1934. In less publicized missions, naval units continued to support scientific missions including survey operations both at sea and via the air.[59] The Asiatic Fleet continued to conduct naval diplomacy in the region with port visits in Japan, French Indo-China, and other Pacific nations, as well as sending a delegation to the funeral of Admiral Togo in Japan in June.[60] Orders for new ships were on the rise, and the Battle Force and Scouting Force continued their annual exercises and the Fleet

Problem doctrine development system. The increases that were anticipated by the Vinson-Trammell Act and the Roosevelt Administration's new, more aggressive views of naval power are often translated to the continued strengthening of the U.S. Fleet, but the Navy's forward presence and crisis response missions remained.

1935

The continuing implementation of the Vinson-Trammell Act dominated the work of the Navy Department in 1935. Increasing the size of the fleet required new budgeting plans and changing views of future naval appropriations. Building the Navy up to the level authorized in the Washington and London treaties, which were still in effect, was one task. However, others began to rise as shipyards began to increase their output. Personnel became a significant issue for the Navy since the new ships would require sailors, and planning for the next year's naval appropriation included discussions of increasing the authorized manpower of the service. In addition, the size and scope of the Naval Reserve were areas that Secretary Swanson was looking to improve. Many older ships were being placed in reserve status but did not have reserve crews to man them. The numbers of ships, sailors, and budgets were all on the rise.[61]

The U.S. Fleet also experienced some adjustments and thinking about the future in 1935. In the previous year, the Battle Force and Scouting Force had been brought together as the U.S. Fleet and crossed through the Panama Canal for the first time as an entire unit. The norm of the previous decade, having the Scouting Force on the east coast and Battle Force on the west coast and having one or the other cross through the canal for exercises and the Fleet Problem either in Pacific waters or in the Caribbean, was formally changed in 1935. The entire U.S. Fleet was kept united as a single force, and Secretary Swanson again added an item to the list of missions for the Navy Department, this time including "to organize the Navy for Operations in either or both oceans." The unified U.S. Fleet, which had ended 1934 in Atlantic waters with ships in Norfolk and making port calls along the eastern seaboard, again moved as an entire unit through the Canal in 1935 and conducted operations in the northeast Pacific, including Fleet Problem XVI.[62] The Navy Department also opened discussion of the need to expand naval construction beyond simply combatants, focusing on the "further great need" of developing fleet auxiliary vessels. The Department identified the current fleet of oilers and auxiliaries as too old, and with insufficient speed to keep up with the Fleet, and suggested a building program running in parallel to the combatants already under construction.

The focus on the U.S. Fleet and the continuing efforts to increase its size, efficiency, and capabilities offered the Navy Department an opportunity to consolidate as well. Bringing the Battle Force and the Scouting Force together created the possibility of also bringing ships from the Asiatic Fleet or Special Service Squadron back into the U.S. Fleet to consolidate combat power. However, the demands of forward presence and crisis response remained key parts of the Navy's mission, and the Department instead left both forward naval forces at roughly the same size that they had been for the last several years.

In the western Pacific, the Asiatic Fleet continued the operations of the two patrol forces. The Yangtze gunboats conducted their convoy operations and independent patrols on the river, and the South China patrol ships continued to work the coast between Guangzhou and Hankou. Operations were largely unremarkable, and insecurity in parts of China still required American presence, but missions were made up of standard patrolling and port visits with no significant crisis response operations. Ships from the Asiatic Fleet made cruises to Japan and French Indochina as well, conducting training as well as naval diplomacy in the form of port calls. Toward the end of the year, after an inspection voyage to Guam, the new Fleet commander Admiral Orin Murfin sailed with his squadron for Australia to represent the United States at the centenary celebration of the city of Melbourne. During that cruise, the ships also made diplomatic visits to the Dutch East Indies and British Borneo. During the year, the Fourth Marines remained in Shanghai and "maintained friendly relations with the Chinese people," while the reinforced Legation Guard remained in Beijing.[63]

Despite the hopes of the Roosevelt administration, stability did not return to Cuba in 1935, and the Special Service Squadron remained in Cuban waters throughout the year. In February, a strike began in the education sector starting with high schools and quickly spreading to the universities to protest the authoritarianism that was returning under President Mendieta and his military backer Colonel Batista. At first, the college students appeared successful, with several of their demands met by the government including the resignation of two cabinet members and increased funding and autonomy for the university in Havana.[64] However, the strike spread to a general strike across Havana and began to show strength in other parts of the country. Mendieta and Batista responded by suspending the constitution, declaring martial law, and deploying the army into Havana's streets.[65]

The CNO reported that the "troubled situation in Cuba continued to be a matter of considerable concern."[66] The United States maintained the same approach to the unrest that it had the year before, keeping naval forces on standby and ready in Cuban waters but largely staying out of the Cuban political upheaval. Under the command of Rear Admiral C.S. Freeman, the Special Service Squadron moved from their permanent base at the Panama Canal Zone to St. Petersburg, Florida. From that temporary base and Guantanamo Bay, they maintained a continuous presence in the waters around Cuba, often sailing off Havana, for nearly the entire year. The troop transport USS *Antares* embarked a battalion of Marines that were kept in readiness at Port Everglades, Florida, in case they were needed either to reinforce the Marines at Guantanamo or for operations to protect Americans in Havana. When the strike was broken by the Cuban Army and temporary workers at the end of March and beginning of April, the Special Service Squadron expanded its area of operations before finally returning to its base at the Canal Zone. The ships made diplomatic port visits to the Bahamas, Mexico, British Honduras, Honduras, Nicaragua, and Costa Rica during their voyages south. *Antares* remained in a ready state with its Marines until August when it returned the battalion to Norfolk.[67]

The year 1935 initiated something like a calm before the storm, with tensions slowly rising globally that would lead to the Second World War. The Navy's forward-deployed warships and the Marine Corps' expeditions continued normal operations, generally following the patterns that had been established across a decade and a half of forward presence and peacetime missions. The Roosevelt administration remained solidly behind efforts to build up the size of the fleet but also continued to recognize the diplomatic and economic value of maintaining globally deployed naval forces in addition to their efforts to enhance the Battle Force.

1936

The year 1936 found a U.S. Navy on the rise but challenges to international stability on the horizon. The Fleet Problem for the year, concentrated on the Pacific side of the Panama Canal, was focused more on the implementation of doctrine and the familiarization of naval commanders with the defense of the canal, rather than the development of new ideas, operating concepts, or tactics. The U.S. Fleet remained concentrated on the west coast, the Battle Force and Scouting Force together as had been established earlier in the Roosevelt Administration. The operations of the forward-deployed forces in the Pacific and Caribbean followed the pattern of previous years without significant crises to respond to. Yet, clouds loomed on the horizon. In December 1936, the terms of the London and Washington naval treaties were set to expire. When American negotiators returned to London in order to keep the limitations in effect, they were able to gather very little agreement. The Japanese walked away from the treaty system entirely, announcing that they planned to let their participation expire at the end of 1936 and refusing to negotiate or sign the even more limited terms of the second London conference. By the end of the year, only the United States had ratified the new treaty, despite the fact that the British, French, and Italians had all signed on at the negotiating table.[68]

The Navy Department's efforts to bring attention to the personnel and reserve policy challenges looming for the Navy appeared to have been ignored by Congress, and the Secretary returned to the issues in his report for 1936. Likewise, little progress was made on the question of fleet auxiliaries, and the Navy Department's report laid out a more detailed explanation of the challenge for an oceanic power with little logistical capability. Again, the Secretary emphasized the importance of a new building program for the logistics force to match the combatants that were now joining the fleet and the necessary expansion of the personnel in the Navy and the size of the Naval Reserve.[69]

In 1936, Secretary Swanson reported that the ships of the Asiatic Fleet spent the year on their "normal functions." Patrols of the Yangtze and South China coast continued, in addition to regular training and gunnery exercises in Philippine waters. With little crisis response required, the fleet experienced an increase in their diplomatic port visits, with ships cruising to Siam, Singapore, the Dutch East Indies, French Indochina, Hong Kong, Borneo, and Japan throughout the year. The Fourth Marine Regiment and the reinforced Legation Guard remained in Shanghai and Beijing, respectively, providing security "maintained as in former years." Admiral Harry Yarnell took command from Murfin as the year approached its close.[70]

Following their return to their base at the Canal Zone when the Cuban unrest appeared to abate, the Special Service Squadron also had a relatively quiet year. The ships provided support to a landing exercise at the island of Culebra, off Puerto Rico, during the summer. Otherwise, the three ships were dispersed mainly across the Caribbean. They made port calls and diplomatic visits to Barbados, Colombia, Costa Rica, the Dutch West Indies, Guatemala, Honduras, Martinique, Mexico, Panama, Trinidad, and Venezuela.[71]

Efforts by the Special Service Squadron in the waters surrounding Central and South America were augmented by some ships of the Scouting Force, particularly for the purpose of surveying. The USS *Hannibal* and *Nokomis* had continued their multiyear scientific efforts for the Hydrographic Office into 1936, but they were also joined by other ships. In cooperation with the Colombian government, the surveys of the Panamanian coast expanded into northern Colombian waters. Following the end of Fleet Problem XVII, Scouting Force ships also made diplomatic visits to ports stretching along the west coast of South America in support of the Special Service Squadron's regular naval diplomacy missions. In addition, mine layers working out of Pearl Harbor assisted in a survey effort to map Kure Island and the Pearl and Hermes reefs in the Hawaiian archipelago, joined by naval aircraft conducting overflight mapping missions. In addition, ships of the Scouting Force conducted the west coast NROTC practice cruise in 1936, with the battleships *Arkansas*, *Wyoming*, and *Oklahoma* all participating.[72]

President Roosevelt made an official voyage to Buenos Aries in late 1936 to attend the Inter-American Conference for the Maintenance of Peace, as an element of reinforcing his "Good Neighbor Policy" toward Latin America. He embarked on the cruiser *Indianapolis* in November and was accompanied by another cruiser and two destroyers. In addition to the summit in Buenos Aires, the four ships also made diplomatic port calls at Port of Spain in Trinidad, Rio de Janeiro, and Montevideo. The squadron returned to the Charleston, S.C. naval base in mid-December.[73]

Naval aviation began contributing to naval presence missions in 1936 as well. The Navy Department elected to use flying boats and their tenders to make port visits, which had the secondary benefit of testing the ability of the squadron to operate forward from their permanent basing facilities. Efforts were first tested with VP squadrons from the San Diego area, flying to Honduran and Mexican waters and supported by the small tenders USS *Lapwing* and *Teal*. Aircraft and tenders from Pearl Harbor made a similar forward deployment to French Frigate Shoals, north of the main Hawaiian Islands. In February 1936, the tenders *Wright*, *Teal*, *Lapwing*, and *Gannet* sailed for ports in Colombia, Ecuador, Costa Rica, and the Galapagos Islands where they were joined by flying boats from VP Squadrons 2F, 3F, and 5F out of the Panama Canal Zone. The ships and aircraft combined operational exercises with diplomatic activities normally associated with port calls.[74]

With the Marine Corps' occupations in the Caribbean over, the Landing Exercises at Culebra became a significant focus for the Corps in 1936. The organization of the Fleet Marine Force a few years earlier allowed for the focus that prior Commandants had desired but had been unable to attain because of the demands for Marines in crisis response and forward presence missions. In addition to the landing forces gathered at Culebra, the Marine Corps flew Marine Aircraft Squadron 1, based at Quantico and formally attached to the FMF for air support missions, to the exercises. Fifty aircraft from the unit flew to Puerto Rico, making stops in Cuba, Haiti, and the Dominican Republic on their way to and from the exercises.[75] The Marine Corps' development of amphibious doctrine was continuing, and their focus was permitted by the relatively quiet year of both the Special Service Squadron and the Asiatic Fleet.

The relative normalcy of naval operations across 1935 and 1936 was soon going to come to an end. As the Battle Force continued to grow, naval aviation developed and spread its wings, and the Marine Corps' new FMF focused on amphibious doctrine, the forward-deployed ships and units of the sea services were about to experience the rising tensions of global politics firsthand. The peace between the great powers had held for 17 years, but it was not going to hold much longer, and much of the rising tension would impact operations at sea.

1937

Secretary Swanson opened his annual report in 1937 with many of the same concerns that he had expressed in prior reports. Between the new ships commissioned, and those funded and under construction, the Navy Department had largely achieved the goals of the Vinson-Trammell Act and brought the fleet up to the force levels of the Washington and London Treaties. Swanson began making the case for continued construction in an effort to begin replacing the older ships in the Navy, many of which had been sailing for decades. However, manpower continued to be a challenge. Congress had not authorized a sufficient increase in the number of sailors and officers in order to crew the new ships that were coming into commission. In addition, Swanson's repeated requests to grow the Naval Reserve and increase its training budget had also not been heeded. In the effort to build more auxiliary vessels to support the fleet, Congress had authorized eight ships but had only appropriated the money for two of them. The U.S. Navy continued to grow but also continued to have pains with that growth.[76]

The new year introduced new tensions on the world stage, which required naval responses. Across the early years of the 1930s, political tensions had been rising in Spain. In the early summer of 1936, the conflict finally boiled over, and a military coup was launched under the leadership of Francisco Franco, initiating the Spanish Civil War. Several thousand American citizens lived in Spain, but the permanent American naval presence in European waters had ended almost a decade earlier. The Navy Department immediately formed "Squadron FORTY-T" to sail for Gibraltar and the Mediterranean. Rear Admiral A.P. Fairfield was placed in command of the mission, and he broke his flag on the cruiser *Raleigh*, which was completing a refit at Norfolk. The cruiser sailed for Spanish waters in September 1936 and was joined by the destroyers *Hatfield* and *Kane*, and the Coast Guard Cutter *Cayuga*. The squadron entered the Straits of Gibraltar and was based out of French ports as they began collecting intelligence and conducting reconnaissance on the situation.[77]

The war also boiled over in northeast Asia when the Imperial Japanese Army staged the "Marco Polo Bridge Incident" in order to excuse an expansion of their invasion of China beyond their established positions in Manchuria. With troops already stationed around Beijing, under the guise of the 1901 agreement that followed the Boxer Rebellion and allowed the Western powers and Japan to "protect" Chinese railways, as well as troops already in Shanghai after the 1932 intervention, fighting spread through China rapidly after the incident at the bridge in July.[78]

In the first half of the year, the Asiatic Fleet was conducting normal operations similar to the past two years under relatively quiet conditions. Diplomatic and training mission port calls were made across the West Pacific in Java, Singapore, Borneo, Indochina, Hong Kong, the Dutch East Indies, and Japan.[79] In the summer of 1937, as hostilities between the Japanese and Chinese rapidly expanded, Admiral Harry Yarnell was in command of the Asiatic Fleet. He reported to the American Consul in the Philippines that the Japanese planned a "short, sharp campaign" to take over key areas of China. Of course, the Japanese overconfidence and sense of superiority did not prepare them for the reality of what would soon become a protracted fight. This combat was an undeclared war and left the Western powers that were operating in and around China to devise their own approaches to continuing their national missions with the fighting raging around them. Admiral Yarnell fell back on the simple clarity of his mission, as stated by the Secretary in repeated years of Annual Reports, to "protect American lives and interests in disturbed areas" and "to cultivate friendly international relations."[80] Yarnell took up the armed diplomacy and forward presence mission with both strategic and diplomatic skills.[81]

In response to the Japanese aggression, Chiang Kai-shek ordered several divisions of Chinese nationalist troops to Shanghai to attack the Imperial Japanese Army and Navy forces that were still in the city. The Japanese initiated a counteroffensive by sending more troops from Japan, and dozens of ships from the Imperial Japanese Navy accompanied the counterattack. The Fourth Marines, and the ships of the Asiatic Fleet, remained in Shanghai defending Americans there and protecting their sector of the international community. With intense urban combat surrounding them, the Americans toed a careful line to maintain neutrality while also ensuring that neither side went too far to attack Americans or American-owned businesses. The Marines deployed to positions along Soochow Creek as they had in 1932 and began coordinating with the British and other defenders of the International Settlement. The Marines were ordered to use "means other than rifle fire" to hold back either of the belligerents, and lethal force was only authorized as a last resort.[82]

Reports of the fighting reached Washington, D.C. and reinforcements were ordered to Shanghai. The Second Marine Brigade sailed from San Diego in late August. Under command of Brigadier General John C. Beaumont, who had previously served in command of the Fourth Regiment in Shanghai, the fresh Marines arrived on 19 September 1937 and moved ashore. The reinforcements included Battery F of the Second Marine Anti-Aircraft Battalion, as Japanese fighters and bombers flew low over the city. The Fourth Marines had been in their defensive positions for several weeks, constantly exposed to explosions and small arms fire that, while not targeted at them, sometimes went astray. The newly arrived First and Second Battalions of the 6th Marines relieved them in place on 23 September and held the defensive positions for ten days before the rested Fourth Marines returned to their positions. After weathering the fighting through August, September, and October, the Japanese began to solidify their holdings in and around Shanghai and the immediate danger to the Marines began to pass. By February, with an uneasy peace descending on the city, the Second Brigade was withdrawn again, leaving the Fourth Marines to continue the defense of the International Settlement.[83]

Service at sea was not any easier for the sailors of the Asiatic Fleet. Yarnell deployed the entire fleet, 41 total ships, into Chinese waters to protect American interests. Japanese naval commanders announced a blockade and the expectation that foreign-flagged vessels would be boarded to determine their actual nationality and then demanded that the international naval leaders report all of their warship movements to the Japanese for approval. As the Japanese solidified their control of Shanghai and began to expand their army's operations toward Nanjing, they also announced that they had assumed the right to either grant or refuse the right of any other nation to operate on the Yangtze River. Admiral Yarnell was having none of it and assumed what he described as an "assertive and forward-leaning" posture. He announced in a policy statement to the fleet his intention to deploy them "as to offer all possible protection and assistance to our nationals in cases where they are needed." He split up his destroyer divisions and sent American warships to most of the Chinese ports, including a significant contingent to Shanghai harbor.[84]

Yarnell himself arrived in Shanghai aboard his flagship the cruiser *Augusta* on 14 August. The ship took up a mooring on the Huangpu River. Less than 30 minutes after its arrival, an errant bomb from a Japanese aircraft fell just 20 yards from the ship and splashed into the water. Remaining in a constant state of readiness itself was dangerous, as *Augusta* suffered an accidental explosion of an antiaircraft shell on its decks, which killed one sailor and injured another a few days later. In October, a piece of shrapnel from a Japanese attack on Chinese forces flew across the harbor and injured the radioman standing next to Yarnell on the bridge wing of his flagship. American naval vessels throughout Chinese waters experienced similar close calls as they placed themselves in between Americans and American businesses, and the Japanese and Chinese in open combat with one another.[85]

In the Caribbean, operations remained relatively quiet in 1937. The Special Service Squadron remained based at the Canal Zone and conducted "visits of good will" across the Caribbean and the coast of South America. Rear Admiral Charles Freeman, who had commanded the squadron during the Cuban operations in 1934 and 1935, repeatedly lobbied the CNO and the Navy Department to focus the Squadron's missions on presence and "good will" naval diplomacy rather than simply the crisis response that had dominated its use around Cuba. His efforts were largely successful after the Squadron returned to the Canal Zone from St. Petersburg. An aggressive schedule of port visits was initiated to show that when an American ship arrived off the coast it was not only there for coercion and gunboat diplomacy. In 1937, these included port calls in Colombia, the British West Indies, Dutch West Indies, Mexico, Honduras, Santo Domingo, Guatemala, Costa Rica, Cuba, and Panama.[86]

1938

With the dramatic combat in China, the continuing civil war in Spain, and the potential for unrest elsewhere, Secretary Swanson's 1938 annual report dramatically increased the discussion of American forward presence and crisis response operations. Two new "missions" followed the established responsibilities of protecting American lives "in disturbed areas" and continuing "friendly international relations." Swanson was more explicit, also including the mission of "evacuating American Nationals from areas of special danger," as well as "maintain uninterrupted communications with and for American Nations and for our diplomatic and consular establishments." Of seven missions listed for the Navy and Marine Corps in 1938, only two were focused on the preparation for a possible war, and the other five centered on the United States' global responsibilities in peacetime.[87]

In the western Pacific, Admiral Yarnell continued to face the "vexatious military-naval questions" that had begun with the opening of hostilities in what the Secretary termed "the Sino-Japanese conflict."[88] Yarnell's orders to his units, almost entirely deployed into Chinese waters both along the Yangtze and the coast, remained largely the same. Tensions remained high, and the danger was dramatic. On 12 December 1937, Japanese aircraft ran a bombing attack on the gunboat USS *Panay* as it patrolled the Yangtze River. The Japanese claimed it was a case of mistaken identity, but, later in the day, a Japanese artillery officer ordered his men to machine-gun the wreckage and any possible survivors.[89] Word quickly spread across the fleet, and ships took up heightened alerts. A crewmember aboard the destroyer *Bulmer* described being anchored between a pair of Japanese cruisers in Qingdao, the Americans with the torpedo tubes loaded and pointed at the Japanese, and the Japanese with their deck guns loaded, manned, and pointed at the Americans.

The sailor remembered that "if we weren't going to get out, then there were two Japanese cruisers who weren't going to get out either."[90]

Secretary Swanson lauded the efforts of the crew of Panay to save their ship and for their "coolness and deliberation."[91] The immediate tension, and very real possibility of war, passed as the Americans elected to accept the Japanese insistence that it was a mistake. Later that spring, Japanese officials requested that the U.S. Ambassador to China have the navy paint the topsides of all their ships scarlet in order to ensure that mistakes did not happen again. Admiral Yarnell simply ignored the missive. In addition, the Japanese insisted that, beginning in June 1938, all neutral ships needed to evacuate a 326-mile zone along the Yangtze headed upriver from Hankou and make official notification to the Japanese of any warship movements.[92] Again, Admiral Yarnell refused to comply with the instructions, offering a general statement of intent of American warships to transit the river as needed.[93] At the end of June, he embarked on the Fleet's armed yacht USS Isabel, usually used for relief operations, and steamed from Shanghai upriver to Nanjing, right through an area that the Japanese had announced as impassable.[94]

Fighting spread along the river over the summer, and both Japanese and Chinese forces made demands on American warships and other international navies. Yarnell walked a careful line, standing up for freedom of navigation and neutral rights but also being practical when the situation called for it. In July, when Chinese forces mined sections of the river downstream, Yarnell moved the gunboat Monocacy to the southern end of the area where it gathered American and international shipping for protection. However, when the Japanese ordered the ship to move from its location, the Americans refused, citing the mining of the river.[95] In August, American Ambassador Roberts followed Yarnell's example, sailing aboard a Yangtze patrol gunboat from Hankou to Chongqing in defiance of the Japanese instructions baring warships on the river.[96] This kind of constant adjustment and ship movements to ensure the safety of Americans and American business interests continued through the rest of the year.

Tensions ran high between the Japanese and the Americans at multiple levels. American sailors still found opportunities to cause trouble. At Yantai in late July, four sailors were taken into custody by Chinese local police who were under Japanese occupation for drunkenly trying to start a fight with a group of police officers. In a separate incident, an inebriated Japanese police commander brandished his pistol and launched into a long tirade against Americans while in the presence of the American Consul and a group of naval officers who were ashore. In the first case, the situation was resolved with a payment of $55 to cover damaged police uniforms and medical treatment, as well as a promise to discipline the sailors. In the second case, a formal apology from the police commander made in the presence of the local American naval commanders resolved the issue.[97]

As the fighting in China reached something of a stalemate, the Spanish Civil War continued to rage on the other side of the world. Squadron Forty-T remained deployed to the Mediterranean, working to evacuate Americans from the areas impacted by the war. The original ships were relieved in late 1937 and early 1938 by the cruiser *Omaha*, and destroyers *Claxton* and *Manley*, based out of French ports.[98] The ships made patrols along the Spanish coast and moved between French ports including Marseilles, Villefranche-sur-Mer, and Menton, and the North African ports of Tangiers and Algiers.[99]

In the Caribbean, the Special Service Squadron continued the planned efforts at making diplomatic port calls and keeping their operations within the parameters of the Roosevelt Administration's "Good Neighbor" policy. The ships of the squadron expanded their cruising area from the Caribbean to include more of South America in 1938, sailing to Colombia, the Galapagos, Nicaragua, Honduras, Panama, Cuba, Guatemala, El Salvador, the Bahamas, Ecuador, Peru, and Chile.[100] The squadron had shrunk to the gunboats *Erie* and *Charleston*, and a few World War I vintage destroyers, and the collaboration with the State Department on the diplomatic efforts was mixed. Despite their best efforts, the arrival of an American warship still signaled "gunboat diplomacy" rather than "good neighbor" in most of the ports they visited.[101]

Along with combat rising in China, combat also continued in Europe. In March 1938, the German Army entered Austria and proclaimed the union between the two countries. In September, Hitler turned his attention toward Czechoslovakia. Meanwhile, the civil war continued in Spain, and Squadron Forty-T maintained its presence and patrols in the Mediterranean and eastern Atlantic. On the verge of the start of the Second World War, the U.S. Navy and Marine Corps continued to build the Battle Fleet and prepare for the possibility that the conflict might involve the United States. However, while still technically at peace, the requirements for naval crisis response did not abate with the rising expectations of war. President Roosevelt and Secretary Swanson's expansions of the Navy Department's peacekeeping and protection missions continued to thrust the Navy and Marine Corps into the gray zone between war and peace.

1939

With war raging between Japan and the disparate armies of China, and the Civil War continuing in Spain, the end of the second decade of "interwar years" brought with it plenty of conflict. There was more to come. By January 1939, the U.S. Fleet had been based on the West Coast and mainly operating in the Pacific for several years, made up of both the Battle Force and Scouting Force. While it still made sense to focus American naval power on the Pacific, with the Japanese threat looming larger each year, Europe was not stable either. The rise of Nazi Germany, the outbreak of the war in Spain, and expanding Italian adventurism all raised concerns for the United States. Squadron Forty-T, now made up of the cruiser *Trenton,* as well as the USS *Badger* and *Jacob Jones,* continued to operate out of French ports and around Spanish waters.[102] In addition, in January, the U.S. Navy established the Atlantic Squadron of the U.S. Fleet. This new unit brought together some of the ships that had previously been assigned to the Training Squadron authorized by the treaty system, which did not count against the treaty limits, as well as several other ships as new warships continued to flow from American shipyards.[103] The Naval Expansion Act of 1938 continued to build the larger fleet initiated by the Vinson-Trammell Act in 1934, and the number of new ships continued to grow.

In addition to the preparation for possible war, the Navy Department continued to be concerned about its peacetime responsibilities. The new missions that had been included by the Secretary the prior year, including the noncombatant evacuation of American citizens, the protection of communication with those citizens overseas, and collaboration with the State Department and the rest of the U.S. government continued to be pursued in 1939.[104] These mission areas continued to be focused around the western Pacific and the ongoing war in China.

In the second half of 1938 and 1939, the Japanese and Chinese had largely fought one another into a stalemate in China. Japanese aggression and their continued insistence on changing the rules for the international community began to lead to suspicion of their desire to expand even further. Intelligence reports suggested that Japanese agents were becoming active in French Indochina and were fomenting the idea that Vietnamese independence under "Japanese protection" was in the cards. Admiral Yarnell continued his policy of spreading the Asiatic Fleet across Chinese waters, sending the fleet's ships, particularly the destroyers, to reinforce the Yangtze and South China Patrol Forces. The fleet also continued to keep an eye on the region more widely and made port calls to East Indies ports and French Indochina to check on the state of affairs.[105]

In the Caribbean, the Special Service Squadron continued its prescribed policy of spreading the ships around on attempted diplomatic port calls. Ships from the squadron visited Honduras, Nicaragua, Costa Rica, and Mexico, as well as a longer distance trip to the Galapagos and Cocos Islands. The tension between the State Department and Navy Department over the use of the ships continued, as some diplomats did not see much use in the port calls and others continued to request ships visit more often. This was the last full year of the Special Service Squadron's existence. With the outbreak of war in Europe in the autumn of 1939, the Navy began neutrality patrols in the western Atlantic and Caribbean, designed to keep combatants out of the areas surrounding the United States. At first, the Special Service Squadron remained intact and was assigned portions of the patrols in addition to ships assigned to the 15th Naval District and the Atlantic Squadron. By late October, in total two cruisers, four destroyers, and two air patrol squadrons with their aviation tenders were operating out of Guantanamo and San Juan as the Atlantic Squadron's contribution. Reports of U-boats crossing the Atlantic to raid the Caribbean raised the stakes in the Special Service Squadron's area of operations.[106] At the end of the summer of 1940, the Special Service Squadron's ships were formally ordered to the 15th Naval District, and the Squadron ceased to exist. Naval operations were built in the Atlantic over the succeeding year, and American entry into the war seemed the highest likelihood to the Navy.[107]

In late 1939, with the French declaration of war against Germany, *Trenton* departed the Mediterranean Coast of France along with the two destroyers in Squadron Forty-T. After briefly responding to a British merchant who believed that they were being stalked by a German U-boat, the squadron made for the neutral port of Lisbon. Based on the Tagus River, they picked up their patrols of the west coast of the Iberian Peninsula and occasionally sailed into the western Mediterranean. In October, the *Jacob Jones* and *Badger* were relieved by the destroyers *Dickerson* and *Herbert*, who had sailed from the eastern seaboard in early September. Rotations of the ships in the squadron continued throughout 1940 and into 1941.[108]

The year 1939 not only brought the two decades of the "interwar years" to a close but also brought open and declared war back to Europe. It was not long before it officially returned to Pacific waters as well. In late 1939, Admiral Hart assumed command of the Asiatic Fleet from Admiral Yarnell and began to reconsider the wide distribution of his forces. With the fall of France in 1940, and the ensuing Japanese invasion into French Indochina, Hart began pulling his ships back toward Philippine waters and the American bases, where they could exercise together and prepare for the war that Hart believed was on the horizon.[109] After the Special Service Squadron was folded into the 15th Naval District, the Atlantic Squadron's Neutrality Patrols grew beyond patrols to begin including convoy duty and submarine hunting over the coming year. Expanded basing in the Caribbean led to wider patrolling and eventually the engagement of several German submarines.[110] The U.S. Navy rapidly began shifting from its peacetime and forward presence missions toward a war footing.

Notes

1 "Report of the Secretary of the Navy," in *Annual Reports of the Department of the Navy, 1930* (Washington, DC: Government Printing Office, 1931), 2–4.
2 "Report of the Secretary," 1930, 4.
3 "Report of the Chief of Naval Operations," in *Annual Reports of the Department of the Navy, 1930* (Washington, DC: Government Printing Office, 1931), 99–100.
4 "Report of the Secretary," 1930, 4.
5 "Report of the Major General Commandant of the United States Marine Corps," in *Annual Reports of the Department of the Navy, 1930* (Washington, DC: Government Printing Office, 1931), 1253.
6 Magdalene W. Shannon, "The U.S. Commission for the Study and Review of Conditions in Hait and Its Relationship to President Hoover's Latin American Policy," *Caribbean Studies* 14, no. 4 (January 1976): 53–71, www.jstor.org/stable/25612723?seq=1.
7 "Report of the CNO," 1930, 100–2.
8 Ibid., 101.
9 "Report of the Major General Commandant," 1930, 1252–53.
10 "Report of the CNO," 1930, 101.
11 "Report of the Major General Commandant," 1930, 1253.
12 "Report of the Secretary," 1930, 6.
13 "Report of the Major General Commandant," 1930, 1254.
14 Ibid.
15 "Report of the Secretary," 1930, 6–7.
16 Ibid., 7.
17 Lucius W. Johnson, "Report on Relief Work in the Santo Domingo Disaster," *United States Naval Medical Bulletin* 29, no. 1 (January 1931): 15.
18 "Report of the Secretary of the Navy," in *Annual Reports of the Department of the Navy, 1931* (Washington, DC: Government Printing Office, 1932), 4.
19 "Report of the Chief of Naval Operations," in *Annual Reports of the Department of the Navy, 1931* (Washington, DC: Government Printing Office, 1932), 111.
20 "Report of the Secretary," 1931, 3.
21 Ibid., 10–11.
22 "Report of the CNO," 1931, 117–18.
23 Ibid., 117–19.
24 "Report of the Chief of Naval Operations," in *Annual Reports of the Department of the Navy, 1932* (Washington, DC: Government Printing Office, 1933), 106. The Secretary elaborated on reports of the Navy's response to China's flooding in his 1932 report.
25 "Report of the CNO," 1931, 119.
26 Ibid.
27 Renamed Force rather than Fleet earlier in the year based on the organizational changes brought about by the London Treaty. "Report of the Secretary," 1931, 4.
28 "Report of the CNO," 1931, 120–21. "Revolution in Honduras," *The New York Times*, April 20, 1931, 1.
29 "Report of the CNO," 1931, 121–22.
30 "Report of the Major General Commandant of the United States Marine Corps," in *Annual Reports of the Department of the Navy, 1931* (Washington, DC: Government Printing Office, 1932), 1161–62.
31 "Report of the CNO," 1931, 120–22.

32 Ibid., 122.

33 Ibid., 125.

34 "Report of the Secretary of the Navy," in *Annual Reports of the Department of the Navy, 1932* (Washington, DC: Government Printing Office, 1933), 3–4.

35 "Report of the Secretary," 1932, 6.

36 "Report of the CNO," 1932, 105.

37 Ibid., 106.

38 Ibid.

39 Ibid., 107.

40 Ibid., 106–8.

41 "Report of the Major General Commandant of the United States Marine Corps," in *Annual Reports of the Department of the Navy, 1932* (Washington, DC: Government Printing Office, 1933), 1159.

42 "Report of the Major General Commandant," 1932, 1159. Hoyt, *The Lonely Ships*, 119–20.

43 "Report of the Major General Commandant," 1932, 1158–59.

44 Ibid., 1160–61.

45 Ibid., 1163.

46 *Annual Report of the Secretary of the Navy, 1933* (Washington, DC: Government Printing Office, 1933), 2.

47 *Report of the Secretary of the Navy, 1933*, 8.

48 "United States Naval Policy," Appendix; *Report of the Secretary of the Navy, 1933*, 34–36.

49 *Report of the Secretary of the Navy, 1933*, 11.

50 "Annual Report of the Chief of Naval Operations," 1933, 10–11. Tolley, *Yangtze Patrol*, 220–21.

51 *Report of the Secretary of the Navy, 1933*, 11. Bernard C. Nalty, *The United States Marines in Nicaragua* (Quantico, VA: Historical Branch, Headquarters, U.S. Marine Corps, 1961), 34.

52 *Report of the Secretary of the Navy, 1933*, 12.

53 *Annual Report of the Secretary of the Navy, 1934* (Washington, DC: Government Printing Office, 1934), 2–3, 7.

54 *Report of the Secretary of the Navy, 1934*, 9. "Annual Report of the Chief of Naval Operations," 1934, 14–15.

55 *Report of the Secretary of the Navy, 1934*, 9. DANFS, Fulton III.

56 *Report of the Secretary of the Navy, 1934*, 9–10.

57 Ibid., 10. Dana G. Munro, "The American Withdrawal from Haiti, 1929–1934," *The Hispanic American Historical Review* 49, no. 1 (February 1969): 1–26.

58 *Report of the Secretary of the Navy, 1934*, 10. Ada Ferrer, Cuba: An American History (New York: Scribner, 2021), 235–247.

59 *Report of the Secretary of the Navy, 1934*, 7.

60 Ibid., 9.

61 *Annual Report of the Secretary of the Navy, 1935* (Washington, DC: Government Printing Office, 1935), 2–4.

62 *Report of the Secretary of the Navy, 1935*, 7.

63 Ibid., 8.

64 Hubert Herring, "Cuba Under Army Rule," *Current History* 42, no. 3 (June 1935): 303.

65 J.D. Phillips, "Cuba is Paralyzed by Strike," *The New York Times*, March 12, 1935, 1.

66 "Annual Report of the Chief of Naval Operations, 1935," 7.

67 Ibid.
68 *Annual Report of the Secretary of the Navy, 1936* (Washington, DC: Government Printing Office, 1936), 4.
69 *Report of the Secretary of the Navy*, 1936, 2–3.
70 Ibid., 8. "Annual Report of the Chief of Naval Operations," 1936, 6.
71 *Report of the Secretary of the Navy*, 1936, 8.
72 Ibid., 7–8.
73 *Annual Report of the Secretary of the Navy, 1937* (Washington, DC: Government Printing Office, 1937), 8.
74 "Annual Report of the Chief of Naval Operations," 1934, 7–8. *Report of the Secretary of the Navy*, 1936, 9.
75 *Report of the Secretary of the Navy*, 1936, 10.
76 *Annual Report of the Secretary of the Navy*, 1937, 1–4.
77 *Report of the Secretary of the Navy*, 1937, 9. DANFS, Raleigh III. "Annual Report of the Chief of Naval Operations," 1937, 7.
78 *China Area Operations Record, July 1937-November 1941*, Japanese Monograph No. 70 (Washington, DC: Department of the Army, 1958), 1–4, http://ibiblio.org/hyperwar/Japan/Monos/pdfs/JM-70/JM-70.pdf.
79 "Annual Report of the Chief of Naval Operations," 1937, 7.
80 *Report of the Secretary of the Navy*, 1937, 7.
81 Stires, "They Were Playing Chicken," 145.
82 James S. Santelli, *A Brief History of the Fourth Marines* (Washington, DC: Marine Corps Historical Division, 1970), 19.
83 Santelli, *A Brief History of the Fourth Marines*, 19. *Report of the Secretary of the Navy*, 1937, 17.
84 Stires, "They Were Playing Chicken," 147–48. *Report of the Secretary of the Navy*, 1937, 7. "Annual Report of the Chief of Naval Operations," 1937, 7.
85 Stires, "They Were Playing Chicken," 149.
86 Donald Yerxa, "The Special Service Squadron and the Caribbean Region, 1920–1930: A Case Study in Naval Diplomacy," *Naval War College Review* 39, no. 4 (Autumn 1986): 68–69.
87 *Annual Report of the Secretary of the Navy, 1938* (Washington, DC: Government Printing Office, 1938), 7–8.
88 *Report of the Secretary of the Navy*, 1938, 8.
89 Masatake Okumiya, "How the Panay Was Sunk," *U.S. Naval Institute Proceedings* 79, no. 6 (June 1953). Stires, "They Were Playing Chicken," 158, fn 44.
90 Quoted in Stires, "They Were Playing Chicken," 149–50.
91 *Report of the Secretary of the Navy*, 1938, 9.
92 "Lockhart to Secretary of State, June 11, 1938," in *Papers Relating to the Foreign Relations of the United States, Japan, 1931–1941*, Volume I, ed. Joseph Fuller (Washington, DC: Government Printing Office, 1943), Document 438, https://history.state.gov/historicaldocuments/frus1931-41v01/d438.
93 "Lockart to Secretary of State, June 16, 1938," in *Foreign Relations of the United States Diplomatic Papers, 1938, The Far East*, Volume IV, ed. Matilda F. Axton, Rogers P. Churchill, N.O. Sappington et al. (Washington, DC: Government Printing Office, 1955), Document 171, https://history.state.gov/historicaldocuments/frus1938v04/d171.
94 "Japanese Warning is Rejected by U.S.," *New York Times*, June 14, 1938, 13.
95 "Yarnell to Leahy, July 6, 1938," *FRUS, 1938, The Far East*, Volume IV, Document 175, https://history.state.gov/historicaldocuments/frus1938v04/d175. "Lockhart to Sec State, July 10, 1938," *FRUS, 1938, The Far East*, Volume IV, Document 177, https://history.state.gov/historicaldocuments/frus1938v04/d177.

96 "Roberts to Secretary of State, July 28, 1938," *FRUS, 1938, The Far East*, Volume IV, Document 186, https://history.state.gov/historicaldocuments/frus1938v04/d186.
97 "Roberts to Secretary of State, July 25, 1938," *FRUS, 1938, The Far East*, Volume IV, Document 183, https://history.state.gov/historicaldocuments/frus1938v04/d183.
98 *Report of the Secretary of the Navy*, 1938, 9.
99 DANFS, Omaha II, Claxton I, and Manley II.
100 "Annual Report of the Chief of Naval Operations," 1938, 5.
101 Millett, "The State Department's Navy," 136–37. Yerxa, "The Special Service Squadron and the Caribbean Region, 1920–1930," 69.
102 *Annual Report of the Secretary of the Navy, 1939* (Washington, DC: Government Printing Office, 1939), 11.
103 *Report of the Secretary of the Navy*, 1939, 10.
104 Ibid., 9.
105 Ibid., 11.
106 Yerxa, *Admirals and Empire*, 115.
107 *Report of the Secretary of the Navy*, 1939, 11. Millett, "The State Department's Navy," 137–38. Yerxa, "The Special Service Squadron and the Caribbean Region, 1920–1930," 69.
108 DANFS, Trenton II.
109 Stires, "They Were Playing Chicken," 154. Hoyt, *The Lonely Ships*, 125.
110 Yerxa, "The Special Service Squadron and the Caribbean Region, 1920–1930," 120–22.

Conclusion

From the end of the Great War to the beginning of hostilities in Europe for the Second World War, the U.S. Navy and Marine Corps were forward deployed and conducting peacetime naval presence missions, year after year. The Asiatic Fleet fluctuated in size, anywhere from 26 to 50 ships across the two decades, but always remained a sizable force and was often reinforced by ships from the Battle Fleet from the west coast when an international crisis demanded it. The Special Service Squadron saw even greater changes in its size over the years. As a result, reinforcement from the Scouting Fleet on the eastern seaboard was even more common, but it remained active and was continuously called upon by the State Department for assistance. U.S. Naval Forces in European waters remained incredibly busy throughout the first part of the interwar years, with constant demands on their ships in the eastern Mediterranean. As stability seemed to return to Europe and the Levant, the American commitment to European waters waned, only to pick back up again with the return of political and military instability and the outbreak of the Spanish Civil War. Throughout the 1920s and 1930s, the Marine Corps operated as an expeditionary force responding to crises and the needs of the nation from the Pacific to the Caribbean. Forward deployment of naval forces, presence operations, and their contributions to crisis response, defense of commerce and the international system of trade, and humanitarian relief were all seen as important missions in the interwar years.

During the 1920s and 1930s, the Secretaries of the Navy listed the missions of the naval services for the President and Congress's review in their annual reports. The preparation for war was certainly a key part of the Navy and Marine Corps mission throughout these decades. Yet, it was only one portion of the mission. Across Presidential administrations, and regardless of party affiliation, the protection of American citizens and interests abroad, integrating efforts with the State Department and other government agencies internationally, and the maintenance of friendly relationships with other nations and people were listed as

DOI: 10.4324/9781003409670-4

important and constant missions of the U.S. Navy and Marine Corps. Naval leaders saw their role in the world as one with both peacetime and wartime responsibilities, and they constructed and organized American naval forces and deployable units in order to be able to conduct both types of missions.[1]

The decades between the world wars also mark what Noel Mauer has called the end of the "first informal American Empire." Occupations of Haiti, Santo Domingo, and Nicaragua all have to be understood in the long history of the Monroe Doctrine, Theodore Roosevelt's "corollary" at the start of the twentieth century, and unique, complex, and very real elements of the American Empire.[2] This era also introduced independence to the Philippines and set the stages for the eventual statehood of Hawaii. All of these elements of American history are bound up with cultural and social issues of race and concepts of American exceptionalism and often had long-term results, which sometimes negatively impacted American foreign policy.[3] There have been numerous excellent scholarly examinations of the American Empire, from its economic and political dynamics to the social and cultural parts of American history. However, that has not been the purpose of this brief survey of the interwar years. Instead, the focus has been on a broad view of the operational elements of keeping the peacetime navy engaged with the wider world, chronicling how the Navy and Marine Corps were deployed globally, and what they did while operating forward. Perhaps, Secretary Daniels's goal of a naval service that would "take its place in the front rank of the champions of international justice and healing" was a bit expansive, but analysis of the long-term political and cultural results of the Navy and Marine Corps' forward presence and peacetime operations in the 1920s and 1930s is a project still to be written.[4]

Looking back on two decades of American peacetime deployment, it is valuable not only to examine the operational and logistical conduct of the Navy and Marine Corps but also to interrogate the results. As a result of the Washington Conference's limitations on building additional bases and defensive works in Pacific holdings in the Four Power Treaty, the deployment of ships to the Asiatic Fleet was the primary way to ensure the defense of American positions in the western Pacific. The strategic viability of defending the Philippines may have been a debatable subject, but it was still the Navy's job and it required forward presence.[5] Likewise, enforcement of the often overlooked Nine Power Treaty required naval forces in the waters surrounding China, layered with the historic mission of protecting American business interests and citizens overseas.

Looking back, we might observe that the deployment of the Asiatic Fleet did not stop Japan from ultimately going to war with the United States. However, at the same time, it appears that American naval deployments, operations, and diplomacy in the western Pacific slowed Japanese expansionism and allowed American leaders to gather the information and intelligence that would help prepare for the coming war. Famously, a young Marine Corps officer named Victor "Brute" Krulak collected intelligence on Japanese landing craft during his service with the 4th Marines, eventually contributing the idea of the bow ramp to the development of the Marine Corps ship to shore connectors in preparation for war in the Pacific.[6] However, a slower pace of Japanese expansionism was also critical to giving the naval building programs of the 1934 Vinson-Trammel Act and the 1940 Two Ocean Navy Act time to produce the ships needed for a Pacific war.

In addition, the regular protection of American business interests by the Yangtze Patrol and the wider Asiatic Fleet repeatedly ensured the safety of the American oil industry. In particular, this often meant the security of Standard Oil facilities and ships. The predominance of Standard Oil in the region provided the American economic leverage that Franklin Roosevelt used in 1941 when, in response to Japanese aggression in French Indochina, he placed sanctions on Japan and all but cut off the flow of oil to the home islands.[7] The use of this tool of economic coercion certainly looks suspect with hindsight. Most historians actually point to the oil embargo as a trigger for the Japanese planning of the attack on Pearl Harbor and the introduction of open warfare. However, that hindsight does not negate the value that the Navy and Marine Corps created by ensuring the protection of American economic power in the region.

Finally, the protection of American interests and the safety of American citizens in the moment of a crisis has always been a valuable mission of the Navy and Marine Corps. From the collaboration with American aid organizations in the eastern Mediterranean and Black Sea following the Great War, to the repeated response to minor political crises in Central America in collaboration with the State Department, and to the protection of American citizens in the cities and towns of a war-torn China, the Navy and Marine Corps were the only arm of the U.S. government that could be relied upon for crisis response in the interwar years. These missions certainly did not keep the Japanese from invading China and keep the Italians out of Ethiopia or fascists from starting a civil war in Spain. However, that was not the purpose of these operations. Instead, the protection of American citizens, American business, and American interests has a value of its own, even when it can not be connected to wider geopolitical developments.

In the interwar years, naval presence itself was not considered a mission. Instead, presence was an unspoken condition that was necessary for the kinds of missions that were conducted. Naval diplomacy, humanitarian assistance, ensuring the safety of American citizens overseas, protection of American economic interests, maritime security, and the potential for deterrence all required that naval forces physically be in a region far from American shores. Whether patrolling, responding to events, or proactively engaging with local populations and international navies, naval presence was assumed to be a condition that was part of the job of the U.S. Navy.

Listing "presence" itself as a mission would not enter American naval writing and strategic discussions until Stansfield Turner introduced the label as a mission in his 1974 article "Missions of the U.S. Navy."[8] Turner placed "naval presence" in the top tier of missions, while simultaneously limiting the way in which naval officers, strategists, and even some historians, thought about the subject. Turner's exposition on naval presence focused, much like Edward Luttwak's contemporaneous writing in "The Political Application of Naval Force," on the deterrent effects of naval forces and their potential for what Luttwak called "suasion" of a potential adversary.[9] Focusing on "presence" as a mission in this specific direction, naval scholars were directed away from the multitude of missions conducted during peacetime that might fall under the umbrella label of "presence," which were conducted by American naval forces throughout the era between the world wars.

In the 21st century, the tactical, technological, and doctrinal developments of the years between the world wars are an attractive subject for naval and military policymakers, strategists, and writers.[10] With the rise of China and its rapid naval growth, and the resulting concern over the potential for conflict in the Pacific, some have come to see the 2020s as the start of another "interwar" era. Some of those officers and national security professionals looking to derive lessons from the past follow the conventional narrative provided by American naval historians and determine that the time has come to bring the fleet home, eschew the missions and responsibilities that fall under the umbrella of forward naval presence, and start developing the new doctrines and weapons needed for a 21st-century maritime war. Former Deputy Secretary of Defense Robert Work has written that the inclusion of forward presence as a key mission for the Navy only serves to weaken the force.[11]

Yet, a survey of the interwar years shows that the conventional narrative, focused on training and preparing for war, is an incomplete narrative. The reality of world affairs is that international crises happen, commerce and trade are competitive activities that themselves engender wider conflict and require protection, and forward naval operations have the ability to advance national interests. While some naval scholars have decried the "tyranny" of naval presence, history itself has its own kind of tyranny and a way of revealing crises and conflicts short of all-out war.[12]

In December 2022, the U.S. Congress recognized the peacetime missions and responsibilities of the Navy by formally changing the U.S.

Navy's mission in the law when they passed the fiscal year 2023 National Defense Authorization Act. The law included a new statement, adding the "peacetime promotion of the national security interests and prosperity of the United States" to the prior language, which defined the Navy's need to be prepared for war.[13] This change formally reestablished the balance between being ready for war and protecting the peace, which had predominated in the years between the world wars. Whether the U.S. Navy, the Department of Defense, and the U.S. government can more widely understand and implement this new mission will remain to be seen.[14] Doing so requires a deeper understanding of our naval past, including interwar years of naval presence, as a foundation for how to develop the tactical, operational, and strategic elements of the naval future.

A slavish devotion to preparing for war, bringing the fleet "home" and focusing exclusively on exercises and new technologies, would leave the world and American interests abandoned on a far shore. The potential to deter war, engage in naval diplomacy, and encourage the strengthening of peacetime norms and structures is something that comes from being present in the oceans and seas around the world. These are missions that have been a part of the history of the U.S. Navy and Marine Corps, from 1800 when Edward Preble sailed the frigate *Essex* to the South China Sea to protect American merchants, through the forward presence operations of the interwar years from the Caribbean to European waters to the western Pacific, to modern operations in the 21st century.

Notes

1 Dudley Knox, "Naval Power as a Preserver of Neutrality and Peace," *U.S. Naval Institute Proceedings* 62, no. 5 (May 1937): 619–26.
2 Noel Maurer, *The Empire Trap: The Rise and Fall of U.S. Intervention to Protect American Property Overseas, 1893–2013* (Princeton, NJ: Princeton University Press, 2013), 184.
3 O'Connell, "Defending Imperial Interests in Asia and Caribbean, 1898–1941," 160–62.
4 "Report of the Secretary," 1920, 3–5.
5 Gerald E. Wheeler, *Prelude to Pearl Harbor* (Columbia, MO: University of Missouri Press, 1963), 15–17.
6 Benis M. Frank, *Oral History Transcript: Lieutenant General Victor H. Krulak, U.S. Marine Corps (Retired)* (Washington, DC: Marine Corps Historical Division, 1973), 23–28.
7 Irvine H. Anderson, "The 1941 De Facto Embargo on Oil to Japan: A Bureaucratic Reflex," *Pacific Historical Review* 44, no. 2 (1975): 201–31.
8 Stansfield Turner, "Missions of the U.S. Navy," *Naval War College Review* 27, no. 2 (March-April 1974): 2–17.
9 Edward Luttwak, "The Political Application of Naval Force: A Precis," *Naval War College Review* 26, no. 5 (November-December 1975): 38–40.

10 A few examples of the many articles on this topic in the pages of the U.S. Naval Institute's journals include: Joel Holwitt, "Recapturing the Interwar Navy's Strategic Magic," *Naval History Magazine* 31, no. 5 (October 2017). Gerry Roncolato, "Interwar Naval Experimentation Offers Lessons for Today," *U.S. Naval Institute Proceedings* 143, no. 10 (October 2017). Scott Swift, "Fleet Problems Offer Opportunities," *U.S. Naval Institute Proceedings* 144, no. 3 (March 2018).

11 Robert O. Work, "A Slavish Devotion to Forward Presence Has Nearly Broken the U.S. Navy," *U.S. Naval Institute Proceedings* 147, no. 12 (December 2021).

12 Daniel Gouré, "The Tyranny of Forward Presence," *Naval War College Review* 54, no. 3 (Summer 2001).

13 "James M. Inhofe National Defense Authorization Act for Fiscal Year 2023" H.R. 7776, 117th Congress (2023), Section 913.

14 Mallory Shelbourne, "Bill Defining Navy's Role Pave's Way for Bigger Budgets, Says Author Rep. Gallagher," *USNI News*, December 6, 2022, https://news.usni.org/2022/12/06/bill-defining-navys-role-paves-way-for-bigger-budgets-says-author-rep-gallagher.

Bibliography

Primary Sources

Archive/Library

U.S. *Chiefs of Naval Operations, Annual Reports 1933–1938*, Nimitz Library, U.S. Naval Academy.

Published

Annual Reports of the Department of the Navy, 1920 (Washington, DC: Government Printing Office, 1921).

Annual Reports of the Department of the Navy, 1921 (Washington, DC: Government Printing Office, 1922).

Annual Reports of the Department of the Navy, 1922 (Washington, DC: Government Printing Office, 1923).

Annual Reports of the Department of the Navy, 1923 (Washington, DC: Government Printing Office, 1924).

Annual Reports of the Department of the Navy, 1924 (Washington, DC: Government Printing Office, 1925).

Annual Reports of the Department of the Navy, 1925 (Washington, DC: Government Printing Office, 1926).

Annual Reports of the Department of the Navy, 1926 (Washington, DC: Government Printing Office, 1927).

Annual Reports of the Department of the Navy, 1927 (Washington, DC: Government Printing Office, 1928).

Annual Reports of the Department of the Navy, 1928 (Washington, DC: Government Printing Office, 1929).

Annual Reports of the Department of the Navy, 1929 (Washington, DC: Government Printing Office, 1930).

Annual Reports of the Department of the Navy, 1930 (Washington, DC: Government Printing Office, 1931).

Annual Reports of the Department of the Navy, 1931 (Washington, DC: Government Printing Office, 1932).

Annual Reports of the Department of the Navy, 1932 (Washington, DC: Government Printing Office, 1933).

Annual Report of the Secretary of the Navy, 1933 (Washington, DC: Government Printing Office, 1933).

Annual Report of the Secretary of the Navy, 1934 (Washington, DC: Government Printing Office, 1934).

Annual Report of the Secretary of the Navy, 1935 (Washington, DC: Government Printing Office, 1935).

Annual Report of the Secretary of the Navy, 1936 (Washington, DC: Government Printing Office, 1936).

Annual Report of the Secretary of the Navy, 1937 (Washington, DC: Government Printing Office, 1937).

Annual Report of the Secretary of the Navy, 1938 (Washington, DC: Government Printing Office, 1938).

Annual Report of the Secretary of the Navy, 1939 (Washington, DC: Government Printing Office, 1939).

"James M. Inhofe National Defense Authorization Act for Fiscal Year 2023." H.R. 7776, 117th Congress (2023).

United States Constitution:

United States Naval Medical Bulletin, 29, no. 1 (January 1931).

Databases

Dictionary of American Naval Fighting Ships (DANFS), Naval History and Heritage Command. www.history.navy.mil/research/histories/ship-histories/danfs.html.

Foreign Relations of the United States (FRUS), Office of the Historian, U.S. Department of State. https://history.state.gov/historicaldocuments.

ProQuest Historical Newspapers: The New York Times with Index. https://proquest.com

Secondary Sources

Anderson, Irvine H. "The 1941 De Facto Embargo on Oil to Japan: A Bureaucratic Reflex." *Pacific Historical Review* 44, no. 2 (1975): 201–31.

Armstrong, David. "China's Place in the New Pacific Order." In *The Washington Conference, 1921–22: Naval Rivalry, East Asian Stability, and the Road to Pearl Harbor*, edited by Erik Goldstein and John Maurer, 249–65. New York: Routledge, 1994.

Baer, George W. *One Hundred Years of Sea Power: The U.S. Navy, 1890–1990.* Palo Alto, CA: Stanford University Press, 1994.

Berry, John M. "After the Deluge." *Smithsonian Magazine*, November 2005.

Bradford, James C., ed. *America, Sea Power, and the World.* Oxford: Wiley and Sons, 2016.

Braisted, William R. *Diplomats in Blue: U.S. Naval Officers in China, 1922–1933.* Gainesville, FL: University Press of Florida, 2009.

China Area Operations Record, July 1937-November 1941, Japanese Monograph No. 70. Washington, DC: Department of the Army, 1958.

Cole, Bernard. *Gunboats and Marines: The United States Navy in China, 1925–1928.* Newark, DE: University of Delaware Press, 1983.

Felker, Craig C. *Testing American Sea Power: U.S. Navy Strategic Exercises, 1923–1940.* College Station, TX: Texas A&M University Press, 2007.

Ferrer, Ada. *Cuba: An American Story.* New York: Scribner, 2021.

Frank, Benis M. *Oral History Transcript: Lieutenant General Victor H. Krulak, U.S. Marine Corps (Retired).* Washington, DC: Marine Corps Historical Division, 1973.

Gouré, Daniel. "The Tyranny of Forward Presence." *Naval War College Review* 54, no. 3 (2001): 11–24.

Herring, Hubert. "Cuba Under Army Rule." *Current History* 42, no. 3 (1935): 303–6.

Holmes, James. "Misfit Ships on China's Great River." *Naval History* (December 2019).

Holwitt, Joel. "Recapturing the Interwar Navy's Strategic Magic." *Naval History* (October 2017).

Hone, Trent. *Learning War: The Evolution of Fighting Doctrine in the U.S. Navy, 1898–1945.* Annapolis, MD: Naval Institute Press, 2018.

Howarth, Stephen. *To Shining Sea: The History of the United States Navy, 1775–1998.* Norman, OK: University of Oklahoma Press, 1999.

Hoyt, Edwin P. *The Lonely Ships: The Life and Death of the U.S. Asiatic Fleet.* New York: David McKay Company, 1976.

Johnson, Wray R. *Biplanes at War: US Marine Corps Aviation in the Small Wars Era, 1915–1934.* Lexington, KY: University Press of Kentucky, 2019.

Knox, Dudley. "Naval Power as a Preserver of Neutrality and Peace." *U.S. Naval Institute Proceedings* (May 1937).

Love, Robert W. *History of the U.S. Navy: Volume One, 1775–1941.* Harrisburg, PA: Stackpole Books, 1992.

Luttwak, Edward. "The Political Application of Naval Force: A Precis." *Naval War College Review* 26, no. 5 (1975): 38–40.

Maurer, Noel. *The Empire Trap: The Rise and Fall of U.S. Intervention to Protect American Property Overseas, 1893–2013.* Princeton, NJ: Princeton University Press, 2013.

Merrill, Tim. *Honduras: A Country Study.* Washington, DC: General Printing Office, 1995.

Millet, Richard. "The State Department's Navy: A History of the Special Service Squadron, 1920–1940." *The American Neptune* 35, no. 2 (1975): 118–38.

Munro, Dana G. "The American Withdrawal from Haiti, 1929–1934." *The Hispanic American Historical Review* 49, no. 1 (1969): 1–26.

Murray, Williamson, and Allan Millet, eds. *Military Innovation in the Interwar Period.* Cambridge, UK: Cambridge University Press, 1998.

Nalty, Bernard C. *The United States Marines in Nicaragua.* Quantico, VA: Historical Branch, Headquarters, U.S. Marine Corps, 1961.

Nofi, Albert A. *To Train the Fleet for War: The U.S. Navy Fleet Problems.* Newport, RI: Naval War College Press, 2010.

Okumiya, Masatake. "How the Panay Was Sunk." *U.S. Naval Institute Proceedings* (June 1953).

Rielage, Dale. "Counting the Cost of Learning: 'Learning War: The Evolution of Fighting Doctrine in the U.S. Navy, 1895–1945'." *Naval War College Review* 72, no. 2 (2019): 107–10.

Roncolato, Gerry. "Interwar Naval Experimentation Offers Lessons for Today." *U.S. Naval Institute Proceedings* (October 2017).

Rosen, Philip T. "The Treaty Navy: 1919–1937." In *In Peace and War: Interpretations of American Naval History, 1775–1978*, edited by Kenneth Hagan. Westport, CT: Greenwood Press, 1978.

Santelli, James S. *A Brief History of the Fourth Marines*. Washington, DC: Marine Corps Historical Division, 1970.

Shannon, Magdalene W. "The U.S. Commission for the Study and Review of Conditions in Haiti and Its Relationship to President Hoover's Latin American Policy." *Caribbean Studies* 14, no. 4 (1976): 53–71.

Shelbourne, Mallory. "Bill Defining Navy's Role Pave's Way for Bigger Budgets, Says Author Rep. Gallagher." *USNI News*, December 6, 2022. https://news.usni.org/2022/12/06/bill-defining-navys-role-paves-way-for-bigger-budgets-says-author-rep-gallagher.

Shenk, Robert. *America's Black Sea Fleet: The U.S. Navy Amidst War and Revolution, 1919–1923*. Annapolis, MD: Naval Institute Press, 2012.

Smith, Gibson Bell. "Guarding the Railroad, Taming the Cossacks: The U.S. Army in Russia, 1918–1920." *Prologue Magazine* 34, no. 4 (Winter 2022).

Still, William. *Victory Without Peace: The United States Navy in European Waters, 1919–1924*. Annapolis, MD: Naval Institute Press, 2018.

Stires, Hunter. " 'They Were Playing Chicken'—The Asiatic Fleet's Gray-Zone Deterrence Campaign Against Japan, 1937–40." *Naval War College Review* 72, no. 3 (2019): 139–58.

Swift, Scott. "Fleet Problems Offer Opportunities." *U.S. Naval Institute Proceedings* (March 2018).

Symonds, Craig. *Navalists and Anti-Navalists: The Naval Policy Debate in the United States, 1785–1827*. Newark, DE: University of Delaware Press, 1980.

Tolley, Kemp. *Yangtze Patrol: The U.S. Navy in China*. Annapolis, MD: Naval Institute Press, 1971.

Turner, Stansfield. "Missions of the U.S. Navy." *Naval War College Review* 27, no. 2 (1974): 2–17.

Wheeler, Gerald E. *Prelude to Pearl Harbor*. Columbia, MO: University of Missouri Press, 1963.

Work, Robert O. "A Slavish Devotion to Forward Presence Has Nearly Broken the U.S. Navy." *U.S. Naval Institute Proceedings* (December 2021).

Yerxa, Donald. "The Special Service Squadron and the Caribbean Region, 1920–1930: A Case Study in Naval Diplomacy." *Naval War College Review* 39, no. 4 (1986): 60–72.

Yerxa, Donald. *Admirals and Empire: The United States Navy and the Caribbean, 1898–1945*. Columbia, SC: University of South Carolina Press, 1991.

Index